JUST BASEBALL

A Guide to Navigating the World of Baseball Recruitment for Players and Parents

MIKE JUST

Foreword by Scott Brosius

SPORTS
PUBLISHING

Sports Publishing books may be purchased in bulk at special discounts for sales promotion, corporate gifts, fund-raising, or educational purposes. Special editions can also be created to specifications. For details, contact the Special Sales Department, Sports Publishing, 307 West 36th Street, 11th Floor, New York, NY 10018 or sportspubbooks@skyhorsepublishing.com.

Sports Publishing® is a registered trademark of Skyhorse Publishing, Inc.®, a Delaware corporation.

Visit our website at www.sportspubbooks.com.

10 9 8 7 6 5 4 3 2 1

Library of Congress Cataloging-in-Publication Data is available on file.

Cover design by Tom Lau
Cover photo credits: iStock

ISBN: 978-1-68358-084-3
Ebook ISBN: 978-1-68358-085-0

Printed in the United States of America

This book is dedicated to my parents, Dr. Anthony and JoAnn Just, who raised me in the game, dealt with the ups and downs, and traveled the country to support me; my sister Danielle Just, who has ALWAYS been there for me; my extended family members who made trips or listened at home to the radio broadcasts; friends and teammates who were there to mentor and advise me along the way; my loving wife, Brittany, who encouraged me to follow my dreams; our boys at home—Dylan and Jack, you can do all things through Him who gives you strength; and the players I train and form lifelong bonds with. I hope it inspires and helps the new generation of ballplayers and leads them on their own unique paths to success.

CONTENTS

FOREWORD

Scott Brosius

From the time I was four or five years old, all I ever wanted to be was a baseball player. I was Johnny Bench in my backyard. I spent hour after hour playing, imagining I was hitting a home run in the World Series, or robbing a home run at the fence. Sound familiar? How many of you thought you might play in the majors, or have kids who dream of a pro career? But all of us hear the numbers and know the odds are against us. Less than one-half of 1 percent of all high schoolers will ever get the opportunity to play professionally. Once a professional, only 10 percent will ever see even one day in the big leagues. But I never wanted to hear those numbers. I watched games on TV and remembered every one of those players was once a kid just like me. They had the same dreams I did. And even though the odds were against me, I realized that someone had to make it, so why couldn't it be me?

I was one of the fortunate few who was able to fulfill my dream of being a major-league player. I was undrafted out of high school, and a low 20th-round pick out of college. I had to work my way through every level of the minor leagues, and spend three seasons on the shuttle between Triple A and the big leagues before I got there to stay. But each player's path is unique. There are so many variables in baseball. Some kids physically mature sooner than others; kids develop at different rates. Most need college baseball, but the gifted few end up in the big leagues just a couple years out of high school. Unfortunately, for every success story we read about, there are a thousand other guys whose careers did not play out like they hoped. So the question becomes: What do we do? How do we put ourselves or our kids on the right path to succeed?

As I told all the other major leaguers I played with, somewhere along the line I made a decision that put me in the best place to have success. I chose to go to a small college out of high school because I felt it was a better fit for me socially and academically, and I'd have a better chance to be on the field and developing earlier in my college career. I look back and realize this was the most important decision I ever made. It paved the way for me to have that professional opportunity and to succeed once I had the chance.

Mike's baseball experience was different than mine, and that is what is so important to understand. There are many different paths, and even more important decisions to make along the way. Often players or parents make the wrong decision simply because they do not have the right information or do not understand their options. What should I do with my 10-year-old who can't get enough baseball? Where should high schoolers play in the summer? What are all the post–high school options? This book can help answer questions you may have, and make you aware of some questions you didn't even know to ask. So I highly recommend you read *Just Baseball*, look at your own situation honestly, and let this book help you make a great decision about your or your child's future career.

PREFACE

The dream . . . it is inescapable . . . We have all had it, at least anyone who has stared down the pitcher, raised the bat, and run the bases, whether they were rubber, corners of cars, grassy patches in the yard, or the neighbor's trees. You approach the plate, tap your shoes with the bat, and then for a moment it happens—the dream. During a game of catch your mind wonders and it happens—the dream. It is not the same for everyone, because sometimes it is just about the hit. Sometimes it is about a home run. Sometimes it is about making the varsity team. But then there are the times when it is about making it to the pros.

Millions of young people run headlong down a path that can be arduous, expensive, and filled with disappointments, especially given that fewer than 1 percent of high school players ever wear a professional uniform. My goal with this book is to spare parents and kids the pain, financial drain, and frustrations I have experienced and have watched others endure throughout my professional coaching days. This book provides an insider's perspective of the baseball industry, including its secrets, politics, and strategies. This practical guide will equip parents and players to make the best decisions for their situations, while encouraging and inspiring all to a greater love for the game.

The game is not what it used to be. It is no longer *just* baseball.

CHAPTER 1
WHY THIS BOOK?

I took the road less traveled by and that has made all the difference.
—Robert Frost

At all levels of baseball there are obstacles along the way that may steer a young ballplayer off his path, while he spends a large amount of money in the process. It's sort of like a game of Chutes and Ladders when you are gaining ground on the board, but you still may fall down the chute. There is so much involved, and some of it is not at all how you think it would be. From the tryouts to the recruiting process for high schools, colleges, and the pros, it's a dream for you or your child, but can be a business for others involved.

People want to believe that the most talented players will rise to the top of the baseball world and stay there. There are a plethora of reasons why this may or may not be the case. There will always be a few phenoms who are destined to make it to the majors. But for others, it's more of a crapshoot, and extenuating circumstances can prevent high-caliber players from climbing up the ladder.

College coaches, high school coaches, injuries, competition, politics, and more (including talent, hard work, and perseverance) all play a role in the process.

So what does it take to make it?

Are you willing to take a hard look at your current situation and view your chances honestly?

I believe it's fair for you to know a little about me to put the advice I give in this book in context. This way, you can understand that I have been through it all, every step of the way, and can use my life experiences for your gain.

I grew up in baseball. At age two, I was hitting a balloon, then, at three, a Nerf ball. At four, I played tee ball, and when I was five, I was playing organized games with seven-year-olds with their parents pitching. When I was seven, I was playing with eight- and nine-year-olds. My parents started me young in baseball and in school, and looking back, it was the best thing to do to prepare me for my competition down the road.

It works quite the opposite today, with so many parents holding their kids back to allow their children to be the oldest in the class. There's nothing wrong with holding a child back if the circumstances warrant it. In fact, I encourage it as long as you follow the rules of your state! If your son is one of the oldest, then you are giving him an advantage mentally, socially, and physically. There are, however, circumstances where you shouldn't hold your child back. If he dominates his grade in baseball and is superior to boys his age, and you are certain he has the ability to play at a high level in high school and, potentially, in college, then keep him where he is. When he is draft-eligible, scouts will look at him and realize they have an extra year to develop him, so they may rank him higher than players who are one year older. In our New England area of the country, it's very common for parents to have their kids repeat 8th grade in order to give their kid an advantage for high school playing time and increase college scholarship opportunities. It's not becoming an epidemic just yet, but it's close. In fact, in 2015 a New Jersey state senator introduced a bill that would have penalized athletes who repeat a grade in middle school in order to gain athletic advantage in high school. Before

Mike is seen here rooting on his clients from the sidelines of his alma mater with his beloved high school freshman coach Paulie Ramasco. *Photo courtesy of Glenn Toepert.*

it was illegal, I encouraged the hold back for two parents because both their sons were decent players and had the potential for better opportunities if they gave themselves another year to mature. One player is now being recruited by Notre Dame and the other is still young but has a private school lined up to repeat 8th grade and he will benefit from it as well, but each case is unique.

I attended a Catholic high school, St. Joseph Regional in Montvale, New Jersey, because it was well known nationally for its baseball program. From there, I went off to Division I, Liberty University, where I would eventually be signed into Independent pro ball. After two years in "Indy" ball, I signed my first affiliated professional baseball contract with the Houston Astros. From there, I found myself back in Indy ball.

What happened?

I was able to succeed in college and in the Independent leagues, but why wasn't I able to move up the ladder?

One would assume that if I succeeded then "they" would find me, right?

That's what I was groomed to believe.

I couldn't have been more wrong. . . .

Baseball is an amazing game: for the camaraderie with the other players, the competition, learning from the best, and strategy. You have to outthink your opponent when it's just you and him. He's on the mound trying to outsmart you, yet you are hitting to outsmart him, and it's all up to you to make the decision on your own. The strategy and camaraderie are my favorite parts of the game and can only be appreciated fully upon experience. You can learn a lot from these interactions; baseball can help you learn how to cope with tough situations and make decisions in your life outside the game.

I got to see the world while playing baseball too. I disliked some of the long road trips, yet enjoyed many others, and the same went for the sleeping conditions. Sometimes we would stay at a five-star hotel, yet most of the time we would sleep wherever possible, which sometimes was on the bus throughout the night. It all depended on the league we were in at the time. Some good coaches etched a memory forever, while bad coaches came and went, but as a whole, the game has blessed me tremendously.

There are some pitfalls to baseball just as any other job in real life; either you face them head on or you run from them.

Many baseball fans have grown up reading inspirational stories and watching movies that all carry the same implicit message: Talent and hard work are the only factors that determine who rises to the top of the baseball world. But the reality of baseball in the twenty-first century is far more complex, and it's important for you to be prepared for the obstacles you will encounter along the way!

I'm going to describe in detail the things you need to know at various steps in your playing career. This will allow you to place yourself in the best situation possible to help navigate your future. To do this, I will take you through my career, show you where I went right, where I went wrong, what you need to do and at what age to do it, and how you can learn from my gains and my mistakes. So suit up, tighten your laces, and let's embark for this field of dreams.

CHAPTER 2
SO MANY CHOICES—
LEAGUES, CLUBS,
SCHOOLS, ETC.

You have a brain in your head. You have feet in your shoes.
You can steer yourself in any direction you choose.
—Dr. Seuss

There are a myriad of choices and questions that can overwhelm you as you become more involved in the world of baseball. How young do I start? How do I know which leagues are good? Which high school? Does it matter? This chapter begins to provide some answers and insight on specific topics including coaching, competitiveness, peer talent, position, and aspirations. It will be said over and over again in this book: *The decisions you make need to be what is best for your circumstances.* Your situation is informed by factors such as talent, passion, and geographical offerings.

How Young Do I Start?

This is one of those questions whose answer really depends upon who you ask. Some would say that you are never too young to have a bat in your hands—just ask my parents. In my house life revolved around baseball; my parents were baseball fanatics. They put a bat in my hand at the age of two. The good thing about it

Mike Just age four. *Photo courtesy of JoAnn and Anthony Just.*

was that handling a bat became second nature. As a kid, batting practice was always in the backyard. My mom was my favorite pitcher, and I now realize how wonderful our neighbors were since hitting their house was counted as a double, and for some reason, all parties involved were okay with this.

Parents, if baseball becomes an interest for your child then cheer him on. Again, my parents fanned my passion by giving me batting practice and being willing to always play catch. Time logged in the backyard allowed me to acquire hitting and ball skills, which in turn gave me a greater sense of enjoyment for the game.

Letting your kids play baseball as early as possible lets them experience the game. The game is meant to be fun. Please, please do not make it a job for them at an early age. If they enjoy the game, they will learn more while experiencing camaraderie with other kids, friendly competition, and simple strategy. These things help a young player decide whether or not baseball is a sport worth pursuing.

Once on a team, if your player gets "called up" by an older team who is shorthanded, encourage them to play, if you believe he can handle it emotionally. Even if there is the chance of feeling overmatched, it is a good thing to get exposed to stiffer competition. This will inspire him to work harder, and where there is success—a hit, a good fielding play, a stolen base, etc.—it will serve as a great confidence booster.

You know your child best and every kid has a different personality, which will inform whether or not playing with older students is a good idea. Your child may experience failure, which is not a bad thing.

I remember taking my first live pitch at age seven when most other players were eight and nine. I felt so intimidated. My goal was to take a walk every time. Soon, my parents realized what I was doing and really encouraged me to start swinging by bribing me with a hermit crab for every hit (my interest at the time). Not only did I begin to swing, but eventually I began to connect and ended the season with an average around .900. I ended up with an insane amount of hermit crabs; however, I had figured out hitting, at least for a seven-year-old, and no longer would I shy away from playing in an older age bracket.

The next year I was again called up to play with the 11- and 12-year-olds for a day. At the time I was nine, and the whole intimidation thing raised its ugly head again because I was staring down a 12-year-old pitcher. I immediately thought I could take a walk, but then I remembered my parents' encouragement, which inspired me to be more aggressive and swing away. The pitch came, and I swung hard and lined the ball over the first baseman's head just inside the foul line.

This opportunity was a turning point for me. As I returned to play with my own age group, I had the confidence to just play hard. It can be difficult to build confidence at a young age. This experience taught me that there is a great deal of excitement and personal satisfaction from getting a hit and scoring runs—a kind of joy and fun rush that is thrilling.

I have a client who had a birthday in September but was pushed ahead to play up in the grade ahead from eight years old. He was entirely overmatched for years, but his parents felt they were doing the right thing by him because he was gaining better experience. Little did they know they were shattering his confidence and although the parents were thinking big picture, the child was not and his heart was barely in it. He only had three hits all season in 8th grade at this point and almost gave up on baseball. I had a long and difficult conversation with the parents and they took my advice to let him repeat 8th grade and furthermore play "down" in the player's mind yet equal with players his age. With that change came instant confidence that bred instant success. The following year he hit .450, his career continued to soar, and he ended up playing college baseball at the D1 level. Without that abrupt change to instill confidence with players his own age, this player's career probably would have ended as a high school back up. Knowing your child and his ability plays a vital role in whether or not he can handle being pushed ahead, held back, or just left alone.

How Do I Know Which Leagues Are Good?

Talent pools vary from league to league and from area to area. Attend a tryout and try to establish some connections. Begin asking around about the different leagues and which ones people recommend. Allow your son to participate in a tryout so he can play in some sort of competitive spring, summer, or fall league.

Tournaments are wonderful places to gain exposure within the baseball community. Equally as important as exposure is playing time. Tournaments significantly increase a player's amount of playing time because you need your whole team somehow, someway to pull together in a weekend that may consist of four or more games. Pitchers will always be a necessity come tournament time. There is no substitute for actually playing games. The more games logged, the more opportunities for the player to build his baseball IQ and improve his game.

It is good to get a handle on which tournaments are the better ones in your area. Again, talk to different people and you will gain a sense of the pecking order. Across the nation for 12-year-olds the top tournament is Cooperstown Dreams Park and Cooperstown All-Star Village. Other significant tournaments heavily scouted along the East Coast are Ripken, Baseball Heaven, and Diamond Nation. The Perfect Game Tournament that is predominantly held in Georgia and Florida also attracts a large pool of talent and, in turn, a significant number of scouts.

Club ball tends to be more serious, with highly committed players who share the goal of competing at the next level. For some this becomes their primary outlet for highly competitive ball. Players are pulled from surrounding towns, counties, and even other states. Travel ball is a more relaxed environment and it's not unusual to find a parent or two involved in coaching. It is mostly made up of players from the same town and, on occasion, a few players from surrounding towns. However, each town is different and may have an extremely competitive travel team to offer as well. It's important to find out these answers by asking your baseball commissioner these sorts of questions to have him point you in the right direction. Club teams, however, usually travel to more tournament venues than travel teams.

Playing in a competitive league with tournaments will reap many benefits. However, a competitive team is only beneficial if there is ample playing time. If you are sitting on the bench continuously and have higher baseball aspirations, then this situation is not a good investment of your time, energy, or money.

Some towns also offer recreational baseball too. Usually "rec" is more laid back than the travel and club realm and allow for all talent levels to join. Again, some towns can be more competitive than others, so ask some questions and do your research accordingly.

If you know which high school your son will attend, the baseball coach there can be a good source of information. Coaches will usually have an opinion about which leagues are good. This is strong advice worth taking. Ask around to make sure that the coach does not have some hidden agenda as to why he is pushing a particular team or league and make sure he is genuinely interested in seeing how you fare with the specific competition he is recommending.

You need to research which program is also the best fit for your family. Dedication, desire, caliber of play, and financial resources are all factors that should be in the mix as you consider your options. Looking at the trips involved for the club or travel team will allow you to evaluate and balance your commitment level and use of resources. Assessing these things is something that should be done every year. As a player grows and matures, his interests, goals, and desires can change, so an annual review is an important exercise.

Which High School? Does It Matter?

You will need to consider numerous factors when choosing schools. I will discuss the importance of good grades in the next chapter, but academics are important when thinking through your high school selection. Finding the right balance is the goal for the student-athlete. For example, perhaps you have been in public education up until high school, but private high school teams provide greater exposure in the world of baseball, but potentially could create other issues academically and socially. Each school and program is unique, whether it be private or public, so each must be assessed very carefully when taking the top schools of your choice into consideration. Moving in the other direction—private middle school to public high school—could also lead to problems.

At this juncture, both the player and parents need to be brutally honest with themselves regarding their aspirations and talent. Do you want to play at the college level? Do you want to play beyond college? Do you have the talent to play at a higher level? Do you have the commitment to put in the hard work needed to improve your game? Do you have the capacity to improve your game and at the same time to make good grades? Do you have the grades to be an asset to a college team? Do you have the grades and talent to attract schools? Have you played enough to spark interest from scouts and coaches? How consistent is your fielding, hitting, pitching, etc.?

It can be difficult for parents to be objective as well as for a player to evaluate his own talent in an unbiased manner. However, there are outside objective standards that can inform your assessment. Ask questions that others are already answering for you, such as: Do I start every game? What are my baseball stats—hits, steals, runs batted in (RBI), errors? How many quality at-bats do I string together? Do I hit the ball hard roughly 7 out of 10 times? If a pitcher, what's my earned-run average (ERA)? How many strikeouts do I average per inning? How talented is my team? How do I rank in terms of talent relative to my own team and my particular position on the team? How competitive is the league or conference I play in? Do I have the talent to start for a premier high school program?

Just because you have good mechanics and hit line drives consistently, doesn't automatically warrant you a position at an elite program. Many variables such as size, arm strength, fielding footwork, and excelling at one or multiple positions, in addition to other variables, can make or break your chances. Why size plays a factor, especially going into an elite high school program, is because even if you do everything correct (as one example) your exit velocity off the bat is 50 mph as a freshman, your chances are very limited as a hitter. A player who may not be as polished mechanically or may be equally polished but showcases an exit velocity of say 75 mph stands a greater chance for offensive success. Why this is the case is because provided each player showcases equal line-drive consistency, the player who hits the ball harder has a greater chance for it to not be caught. In addition, he can rack up extra base hits. A smaller player who has yet to mature physically has a lesser chance to compete against a larger, more mature player of similar ability. This isn't always the case. I was 5'4" during my freshman year of high school (one of, if not the smallest on the team) and I batted .505 and received the MVP of our freshmen team, so it's possible for sure to get a chance to compete, but it's nevertheless not as common. Not to state the obvious, but the one issue that cannot be overlooked is playing time. It does not matter what program, club, team, or school your son plays for, if he sits on the bench, he is not getting critically important experience. To go to the next level he needs (at a minimum) to be an everyday player for either his school or club or travel team. A day off every now and again won't hurt him, but he needs to be in the lineup most of the time.

Always consult the coach of the team to find out who will be playing where and how your player will fit into his game plan. Listen carefully to what the coach says and read between the lines. Sometimes our own bias for our children can get in the way of how we listen. Be smart about how you interpret what is communicated. If you ask about open slots in the infield for next year and the coach responds, "Well, we have a solid infield right now and into next year, but you never know," what this statement really means is, "I am not changing my infield unless someone gets hurt or transfers, so either your player goes to the outfield or becomes a backup infielder."

As with many things in life, being in the right place at the right time is essential. If there is a player coming in who has been recruited—even though in high school players are not supposed to be recruited—he will play. There are lots of ways not to recruit a player but still communicate interest. Being cordial and showing interest in an 8th-grade catcher who has lots of talent is just one of those ways, especially if you are a coach who is in need of a catcher next year. If the player is telling you that your program is one he wants to be a part of, then this makes it easier to engage this player without technically recruiting him. If a player has already proven himself to the high school coach, he will probably play.

Back in 2006, when I first started giving pro baseball and softball instruction, I had two players, who we will call Player 1 and Player 2. Both were talented ballplayers and, based on what schools they attended and how much they had improved in their training, I can tell you they both had the potential to hit .500 in a high school season at a competitive level.

One received an opportunity to play at the high school level and hit over .500, and one did not receive an opportunity at all and was cut. The key difference was in the legwork being done by Player 1's parents.

When talking to the mom of Player 1, I learned she and her husband were actively involved in his life. She marketed him to the coach before he went to high school. She brought him to showcases (which I will touch on later) and tournaments all over the East Coast to show off his talents to college teams, and they also went to the college camps. Player 1's parents did anything and everything they could to help their son out, which was commendable. Therefore, the position became his job to lose.

Player 2 was not so fortunate. His mother grew ill and, therefore, could not be directly involved with his life. His father was working hard to support them and it was hard for him to get involved as much as he would have liked. When freshman year came along, Player 2 was cut from the team. He transferred to another school where he could have batted in the top of the lineup, yet once again, he got cut.

I assure you it was not because of talent. He could have achieved All-League and All-County honors. Unfortunately, his parents could not be involved enough to make the necessary connections that would have allowed him to get that proper look.

Both high school programs had their team "set" already. A lot of these coaches get comfortable and they already have their team picked in their minds before tryouts even begin. They're not legally allowed to recruit, but showing an interest in a player without actually asking him or pursing him outright isn't necessarily recruiting. It's just the coach being respectful and answering basic questions, right? It's a gray area, but it never hurts to find out information.

Never make the mistake of thinking that when the coach sees your son in action that he will never take him out of the lineup. This line of thinking is flawed. Your player has to get into the lineup first before he can be taken out of it. Additionally, coaches do not think about filling positions that are already filled. This idea should not de-motivate players, but rather inspire them to hustle more to either confirm the coach's inclination or change a coach's mind in your favor. We will talk in greater detail about the importance of hustle in Chapter 7, but you should never underestimate its value in terms of opening doors and creating opportunities. Frankly, if your family is not well off financially, it may be a hindrance but it should not stop you. This may mean you stand less of a chance to network yourself but it shouldn't stop you from working hard. You may just have to save your money and pay your own way. Attending college camps doesn't cost a whole lot and if you work a weekday or weekend job in the offseason like I did in high school, you can save up enough to cover your expenses for a few college camps and showcases. If you perform well and there's interest from one program, then you got the ball rolling. Before you attend the camp, ask what the camp will entail. If they plan on keeping record of your tools, then while at that camp, ask for information on your results (such as 60-yard dash time, arm strength mph, exit velocity off your bat) so you can save them on file to distribute to other schools as well and save yourself some more money. When you start the buzz with one program, you can play that one off the rest.

A Winning Program

What, if any, are the advantages or disadvantages of a winning high school or college program? For one, a school that wins will receive more notoriety in the county, state, and nation. The more games they win, the higher ranked the school becomes; if you're a starter, this in turn gives you more credibility as a player who is a part of that program.

Secondly, scouts that haven't visited one of your games will have to assume you are playing against quality competition and winning against that competition to get as far as you did, especially if your school is ranked. It is not absolutely essential to choose a high-level high school program, especially with today's summer club teams. But if you know you have the ability and can play at a school that wins, then it will help you prepare your future against the best competition.

According to an online poll, my alma mater, Saint Joseph Regional, was ranked 24th in the nation for the 2017 season.

At our Just Hits facility in northern New Jersey, we have had many players go on to play high school, college, and pro ball. However, three players, in particular, have unique case stories. They worked as hard as our other clients, and we felt they were equally as good. Unfortunately, these particular three were cut from their high school programs, and each program was a different caliber. One was a highly ranked parochial school, one was a highly ranked public school, and the other was a lower-tier public school that was not ranked in the top 25 in the county.

Now, if this scenario happened back in the 1990s or earlier, then all three of their baseball careers would have had a 99.9 percent chance of ending there. Thanks to the club teams and the college camps that have become part of today's game, all three of these players successfully signed contracts at the college level to play and all three fulfilled those commitments and played. They never gave up and we convinced them not to because of the club route, college camps, and showcases.

Just because you get cut doesn't mean the road should end for you.

If that happens, pick yourself up by your cleats, as they did, and find out where you need the most improvement.

Attack that weaker part of your game.

At least you can honestly say you gave it all you had, and then some, regardless of the outcome.

Conversely, some disadvantages of a winning program could be the costs involved through expected commitments, as well as the playing time. Because it is a quality program, more talent will flock to that program, thus making your starting opportunities more limited too.

Look into the qualifications of the coaching staff and the players in front of you before you make a decision to commit to a highly ranked program.

The bottom line is that either a private or a public school could be the best option for you. Both have produced talented players that have advanced to the next level.

As parents, you can help by researching the incoming players and where they will most likely play. Consider how your son matches up with these players. If your student is one of the players that was "recruited" (in quotes because it's illegal for players to actually be recruited for sports at a high school level) and has been guaranteed (keep in mind, there are no guarantees) playing time, then this is worth strong consideration. Opportunities like these are the result of hard work on behalf of a fully engaged player and parents who did their research, who gained exposure through tournaments, showcases (we will touch on these in Chapter 8), and college camps, and who had lots of conversations with potential future coaches and others.

One other scenario to be aware of has to do with a teacher's son who is on the team or a coach's son on the team. Even if the son is mediocre, he will more than likely play. There is a chance that even if he is a weak player, he will play. Do not fall into the trap of thinking that your son is better and so he will play. For the majority of the teams, this is not reality.

Remember, be smart in assessing your situation, your opportunities, and your talent, but don't forget to have fun. Do not lose sight of the balanced approach when making what seem to be exclusively baseball decisions, because there are no decisions that are only about baseball.

CHAPTER 3
PREPARATION CAN
MAKE ALL THE DIFFERENCE

Before anything else, preparation is the key to success.
—Alexander Graham Bell

Someone once said, "The harder I work, the luckier I get. . . ." Preparation is about creating opportunities. As players, we live distracted lives, which then cause us to greatly undervalue preparation and opportunities. As parents, we are distracted by personal and professional responsibilities that bombard us daily. Preparation involves a holistic approach, from cultivating physical habits to adopting strong academic discipline. High school players often underestimate the value of the right strength training, conditioning, and diet. *Right* is the key word here, because what is good for baseball is not necessarily ideal for other sports, e.g., development of fast-twitch muscles vs. slow-twitch muscles.

Most young people are on the cusp of realizing their physical potential in high school, which means learning how best to care for their bodies could play a pivotal role in their on-the-field productivity. Strong academics are also essential for preparation and should not be overlooked. Good grades can create a plethora of opportunities in baseball.

How Do I Prepare Before High School?

First, we're going to discuss connections and reputation. What college or pro connections does your potential high school coach have? If your future high school coach is not well liked or respected by colleges or professional scouts, his opinion probably won't carry much weight. Coaches can do more harm than good. Do your research before you commit to the high school you always wanted to go to.

Don't choose the school because of its colors. You might not know as much as you think you know about the talent level at the school of your dreams unless you have researched what colleges think about that school. How do scouts assess the talent level at your high school? One way to research this without asking questions is to find out who the "phenoms" were of that high school program in the past and where they are now. Were they starters at the college level at some point? Did they sign pro contracts out of that high school? If many "studs" from the high school didn't start at the college level, it's safe to say that you will be classified as a "big fish in a small pond" and you could get lost in the talent pool at the college level. Therefore, choose your high school wisely if your goal is to play in college or the pros.

In New Jersey, the parochial schools usually draw a more competitive talent pool than the public schools simply because a public school has limited access of players from a town or a few towns. In the past, a player hitting .500 at a parochial school would most likely receive All-State honors because of the talent pool he was in, yet a ballplayer hitting .500 at a public school would not necessarily earn All-State honors. For each town and county, the talent level of the competition is a factor in determining awards and honors, with some public school towns defying the odds.

Also, the high school coach can play a big part in determining whether his players receive awards. When I was a senior at a parochial high school, I was an All-State player. My friend went to a local public school where he batted close to .400 and only received Honorable Mention All-League. He was devastated, and this was the turning point of him ending his career rather than pursuing a potential college opportunity. Weeks later, he found out that his coach was absent the night of the All-County meeting and was eventually fired. If your own coach is not defending you as a player, no one else is. This is just one more reason why doing research about your high school program, whether public or private, is essential.

Academics should play a vital role in the high school choice as well. However, if you are motivated enough and the high school has honors and Advanced Placement courses to offer, then in most cases you will be challenged enough in those courses to be prepared for the next level academically.

Importance of Strength Training, Conditioning, and Diet

Strength Training

While in high school, a good weightlifting and running program is instrumental to your success as an athlete. Weightlifting should focus on enhancing your baseball strength, speed, agility, and power. An athlete's physical condition both in and out of season is important. Proper form is the key to success in all facets of the game: hitting, pitching, fielding, catching, throwing, and baserunning.

> **Tip!**
> The key to form is muscular ability.
> In order to master the mechanics of baseball,
> muscles have to be strong and flexible
> enough to get into those mechanical positions.

Functional Movement Screening (FMS), used by many major-league organizations, is one of the best ways to evaluate balance and joint mobility. This is important because organizations can assess an athlete's potential for injury. Teams even negotiate players' contracts based on their FMS screening. According to the Functional Movement Systems company website (www.functionalmovement.com):

The FMS simplifies the concept of movement and its impact on the body. Its streamlined system has benefits for everyone involved—individuals, exercise professionals and physicians.

Communication—The FMS utilizes simple language, making it easy for individuals, exercise professionals and physicians to communicate clearly about progress and treatment.

Evaluation—The screen effortlessly identifies asymmetries and limitations, diminishing the need for extensive testing and analysis.

Standardization—The FMS creates a functional baseline to mark progress and provides a means to measure performance.

Safety—The FMS quickly identifies dangerous movement patterns so that they can be addressed. It also indicates an individual's readiness to perform exercise so that realistic goals can be set and achieved.

Corrective Strategies—The FMS can be applied at any fitness level, simplifying corrective strategies of a wide array of movement issues. It identifies specific exercises based on individual FMS scores to instantly create customized treatment plans.

Before lifting you should always consult a qualified personal trainer in your area to make sure you display accurate form when performing baseball-specific exercises.

Stretching plays a vital role before and after you strength train. If you do an activity such as a treadmill, cycle, or jumping jacks, it will help increase your blood flow to the muscles and allow them to loosen up before your workout begins. You should also include a cool-down stretch at the end of your workout to ensure your muscles don't tighten up as much. This will allow for maximum flexibility and allow you to perform at your highest potential during your next workout.

According to Certified Personal Trainer and former Blue Jays organizational pitcher Ryan Page, "For strength training in general, power equals work divided by time. This is crucial in increasing explosiveness. Exercises such as power cleans, hang cleans, squats, dead lifts, and medicine ball slams are all positive examples of power-building workouts. These exercises can be combined with strength-building exercises such as one-arm rows, walking lunges, and tricep pulldowns to ensure the athlete is training both Type I (slow-twitch) and Type II (fast-twitch) muscles."

Your abdominals are extremely important and should not be neglected during your workout regimen. It's recommended to flex your core in all workouts so you get a partial core strengthening as you conduct both power-building workouts and strength-building exercises. In addition, an isolated 10- to 20-minute core workout should be incorporated a minimum of three times per week. Mixing up the core workout with different core exercises throughout the week will ensure maximum strength in both the upper and lower abdominals while medicine ball twists can include the oblique muscles as well.

A proper well-rounded training schedule is critical for maximum results. This process begins in the offseason and continues throughout the season. During the offseason strengthening phase the goal is to gain strength and power. Strength is gained by increasing the intensity (weight) and lowering the volume (number of repetitions) of the workout. Typical offseason strength-building exercises consist of three to six sets of eight to twelve repetitions.

The preparatory phase of a strength-training program should begin a few weeks prior to the season. In this phase, the athlete should spike the intensity of the workout and lower the volume. The general guideline for the prep phase would be three to six sets of two to six repetitions.

In-season training is extremely important to maintain strength and conditioning. You do not want your body to break down and lose strength during this time. You want to be able to rely on your body for maximum performance. During in-season training, your schedule should consist of more volume (15–20 repetitions) with lower intensity to maintain the gains you've had in the offseason. Plyometrics are a key part of in-season training as well to keep your endurance up.

There are generally three exercise goals to consider: bulk building, strengthening, and muscular endurance. Bulk building consists of two to six repetitions. To strengthen muscles, eight to twelve repetitions are suggested. To increase muscular endurance, 18 to 20 repetitions are required. There are many trainers in the marketplace, yet many aren't qualified for sports- or baseball-specific training. Do your research and hire a good trainer who can improve your speed and power skills that, in turn, will transfer baseball-related workouts to the field. A football trainer may or may not make a solid baseball trainer. If he has you "maxing out" on bench presses and your chest is so large you are less flexible, which is causing you to pull off the ball and not maximize extension through the zone with each swing, then he is training you as a lineman and not as a baseball player. Pitchers need to be especially careful of which trainer they work with. Exercises such as the barbell bench press, chin-ups, and military press are red flags for pitchers due to added strain put on the shoulders. This increase in risk to the shoulders can potentially lead to inflammation, tendinitis, impingements, and other strains or tears. Investigate before you invest or you may end up wasting valuable time and money.

Conditioning

Conditioning for pitchers is vastly different, and considerably more intense, than a position player's running program. When a pitcher is in a game, each pitch is a maximal effort motion. The pitcher also needs to be able to produce quality pitches for an extended number of throws and potentially last the whole game. For this reason pitchers need to combine distance, intervals, and sprint workouts. The sprints will train the fast-twitch muscle fibers and help the pitcher maximize explosiveness throughout each pitch. The intervals and distance workouts will help to build stamina. In addition, long-distance running will help to increase blood flow to remove lactic acid (the by-product created in muscles which causes soreness). Position players should avoid running long distances unless they are working some lactic acid out of their systems. Studies show that jogs over long periods of time train slow-twitch muscles rather than fast-twitch muscles. And after all, when playing baseball, are you ever moving for that long without rest?

Tip!

Notice the word "train" is used rather than "create" in regard to slow-twitch muscles. It's a common misconception that training can "create" fast- or slow-twitch muscles. Studies have shown that training can't create muscles, but instead can increase the cross-sectional area of the muscle fibers, making them more efficient.

Coaches in college and in high school love the mile, two-mile, or 5K to prove a player's work ethic. These runs are less beneficial for baseball players who aren't pitchers. There's a reason why track runners aren't stocky like second basemen. Timed sprints, gassers, or any form of sprint/stride/walk/rest scenario can get you in shape by building stamina while aiding the buildup of fast-twitch muscle groups.

The gassers that got me in the best shape took place over the course of 50 yards. We would run to the 50-yard line and back in under 16 seconds with a 45-second rest period. We would do that six times the first week and increase one more a week until we were doing that for 12 reps consistently while making each time in under 16 seconds. This allows the use of fast-twitch muscles that you will use every day as a position player, while also including a change of direction when you hit the 50-yard mark and a rest phase that coincides with on-the-field activity.

Diet

Your first impression as an athlete is only significant if it's a bad one. Most coaches apply the motto, "What have you done for me lately?" Therefore, good games are easily forgotten when you are expected to perform. Game-winning hits or stellar pitching performances are a whole different story and are memorable for all who witness them. However, if you come into high school 50 pounds overweight and you expect to make the team, if you're at an elite program, your chances of making the roster are thin.

Many good players gain too much weight, and they are the first to get overlooked because they are giving the coach a reason from the start not to play them. If you are not in shape, you are telling your coach you're lazy and that you're not serious about high school baseball. A diet that's high in protein and includes healthy carbohydrates early in the day, combined with proper workouts, will help you get in shape quicker.

Consulting a nutritionist may not be a bad option to get you started in the right direction. Also you should factor in any food allergies you may have when you consider the items listed below.

Have you heard the phrase: "You are what you eat"? Players have been known to feel lethargic when they eat poorly, and some claim their reaction time even slows a bit based on how much, what, and when they eat.

When training in the offseason or in season, you will have greater gains by attaching a proper diet to your workout regimen.

So what do baseball players eat?

- Salads that include but aren't limited to: chicken, tuna, or egg salad with light mayo, legumes, lentils, tofu, other beans, and bean sprouts.
- Protein bars with low sugar content.
- Any and all boiled, steamed, or raw vegetables.
- Any lean beef or steak.
- Chicken.
- Pork. *Avoid the fatty parts or make sure it's prepared with fat dripped off.*
- White albacore tuna. *Avoid bluefin tuna, which contains much higher mercury levels.*
- Wild-caught salmon is high in omega-3 fatty acids. *Farm-raised salmon is not as healthy because of what the fish are fed and sometimes the conditions they are raised in. Women who are pregnant are informed to stay clear of farm-raised fish due to potential health risks to the baby, but are encouraged to eat wild-caught fish.*
- Oysters, mussels, and crabmeat are highest in omega-3 out of all shellfish. *Avoid large consumption of raw oysters, which can contain bacteria.*
- For their size, in ratio to other fish, sardines have the highest content of omega-3 and large protein content.
- All fresh fruit and dried fruit.
- Nuts, especially cashews, peanuts, almonds, and walnuts. *Watch excessive salt.*
- Seeds like chia or flax seed are best. Pumpkin seeds and sunflower seeds are okay in moderation but watch the salt and fat content. One cup of sunflower seeds can contain upwards of 70 grams of fat, and according to Livestrong. com (www.livestrong.com/article/373006-are-sunflower-seeds-fattening/): "Although the majority of the fat [in

sunflower seeds] is heart-healthy polyunsaturated fat, too much means extra calories—and extra pounds."

- Natural sweeteners like Stevia (extract from the leaves of its plant) or honey instead of sugar. *There are different grades of honey quality too.*
- Ginger for natural energy boost.
- Greek yogurts provide a large content of protein and good bacteria. Plain varieties are generally low in sugar. Also look for the low-fat options.
- Egg whites.
- Water, more than what is normally recommended due to the high protein content in your diet.

Tip!

According to http://www.livestrong.com/article/308210-high-protein-diet-water/: "When athletes consume more protein without increasing water, their blood urea nitrogen level (BUN)—rises, Janice Palmer explains in her April 2002 issue of 'Advance.' High protein intake causes the kidneys to produce more concentrated urine . . . a sign of dehydration caused by the extra fluid needed to eliminate waste."

The article also states, "Increasing water intake may also help avoid another potential complication of high protein intake: kidney stones."

- Carbonated water like Pellegrino is okay. *Carbonated water is simply water infused with carbon dioxide.*
- Most juices such as orange, tomato *(watch sodium),* cranberry, pomegranate, grape, or even a mixed juice or smoothie, but watch the sugar.

- Choose Body Armor's lower sugar/lower calorie option for electrolyte replenishment.
- Soy, coconut, or almond milk (unsweetened to reduce calories), but if you have to have regular milk then drink organic milk at the lowest percent of fat content.
- Some gluten-free or whole wheat pastas but watch quantity.
- If you think, "There's no way I'm eating all of the above items consistently and when do I even have time for all of that?," buy a blender or juicer. It doesn't take long to throw a bunch of the items that mix well together in a blender and drink it.

Carbohydrates

There are good carbohydrates and bad carbohydrates, good fats and bad fats, and all play a vital role in your success as a ballplayer. Carbohydrates get a bad reputation as the reason for weight gain, which is only a partial truth. The truth is that good carbohydrates are extremely important in your diet if used correctly. Carbohydrates are what your body uses to produce energy. Any diet for an athlete that recommends no carbohydrate intake at all should be avoided altogether. It is also important to understand when it is okay and not okay to eat carbs. A reverse pyramid theory of time and intake is ideal.

When you wake up in the morning, your body does not have a ton of energy stored. Breakfast should be the biggest meal of the day and contain the largest amount of carbohydrates. When you think carbohydrates, you shouldn't just think bread and potatoes. Keep in mind there are carbohydrates found in fresh fruit and healthy cereals too. Each meal to follow should be smaller and contain a lesser amount of carbohydrates. After lunch and dinner, be cautious of how many grams of carbohydrates you consume. Your body generally expends less energy after lunch and dinner and any carbohydrates not used will be stored as fat cells. Carbohydrates can also be important to eat after a workout to restore glycogen levels in the muscles and help the muscles to recover.

Foods to Avoid or Watch

You don't have to completely weed these out of your diet. Control the intake and assess everything in moderation:

- Watch excessive dressings on the salad.
- Watch excessive sauces.
- Watch dips.
- Avoid candies and chocolates. If you have to have something then choose dark chocolate, which is the best of the bunch.
- Avoid alcohol, *especially beer, which contains lots of carbohydrates.*
- Limit chips.
- Avoid any and all desserts.
- Avoid anything high in sugar.
- Avoid anything that can be high in grease such as excessive helpings of bacon and sausage.
- Avoid certain cheeses. *Some cheeses are higher than others in saturated fats, calories, and sodium. The low-fat or fat-free cheese varieties aren't so bad for you if they're available.*
- Avoid soft drinks and sodas that are high in sugar.
- Avoid butter and oils. If necessary, *use olive or avocado oil instead.*

- Watch your timing and intake of excessive carbohydrates such as bread, potatoes, and pasta dishes.
- Watch processed deli meat. *If you have to, find the all-natural, organic varieties.*
- Be smart and temper everything in moderation.

> ## Tip!
> It won't hurt if you slip up
> every now and then. You may not
> stick to the proper diet 100 percent of
> the time anyway and then you may
> lose your focus thinking that you have failed.
> Don't think of it as a pass/fail test. Think of it
> as a climb with some detours along the way.
> Just keep climbing in the right direction and
> make sure you are using the top list much
> more often than the bottom list.

Why Do Good Grades Matter?

Good grades are essential for opportunities in life, and even more so in baseball.

My varsity opportunity came as a sophomore in high school mainly because the junior in front of me failed two classes. His ineligibility allowed me to step in and earn the spot and stay there for three years.

At each level of the game, grades are there along the way.

For you to gain acceptance into high school honors classes, you must score well on an entrance exam or do well in your middle school classes. Then to maintain honors courses in high

Mike Just's client Peter Chugranis doing his homework. *Photo courtesy of John and Lisa Chugranis.*

school, you must do your work and maintain good grades. The better your grades, the more doors open up for high school and college acceptances down the road. Colleges and universities look at students' grade-point averages (GPAs) when making admissions decisions, but they also give considerable weight to the SAT and ACT. Make sure you research the schools you are interested in and whether they prefer the SAT or ACT, though it can't hurt for you to take both.

Your past curriculum plays a big factor in whether or not you will score well on the standardized tests. If you were never taught it, it's highly unlikely you are going to figure it out during the test. Therefore, consider hiring a tutor to help you get the best score you can.

If you score poorly on the ACT or SAT, many schools will not consider you for scholarships or acceptance. Even if a school wants you because of your baseball ability, bad test results will suggest to the college coach that you might not be able to handle the college workload. The coach may think you could fail out or drop your GPA into a range that would make you ineligible to play. Why cause a stumbling block if you can avoid it?

In some cases tutoring has raised a player's scores significantly. Those extra hundred points could be the difference that will open the doors to many schools that would not even consider you if you were not an athlete.

Tip!
Be sure to not only study hard, but study smart. A best practice while studying is to incorporate a 10-minute break period every 45 minutes or so. You'll find you retain more this way and increase your studying efficacy.

How important is GPA? Only 51 percent of schools can recruit you if your GPA is 3.0. This means you eliminate about half of the schools with a 3.0! Furthermore, fewer than 10 percent of schools are able to recruit you if your GPA is 2.0.

After you're in college you have to maintain a certain GPA as well to be eligible. How high a GPA do you need?

NCAA posts the following on their website, www.ncaa.org/remaining-eligible-academics:

Because intercollegiate athletics is part of the fabric of the university, student-athletes must be committed to academic achievement and the pursuit of a degree.

Student-athletes must meet academic standards throughout their careers on campus to remain eligible to participate in intercollegiate athletics. Member institutions in each division create academic standards specific to that division's goals.

In Division I, student-athletes must complete 40 percent of the coursework required for a degree by the end of their second year. They must complete 60 percent by the end of their third year and 80 percent by the end of their fourth year. Student-athletes are allowed five years to graduate while receiving athletically related financial aid. All Division I student-athletes must earn at least six credit hours each term to be eligible for the following term and must meet minimum grade-point average requirements that are related to an institution's own GPA standards for graduation.

Teams in Division I are also subject to the Academic Progress Rate (APR), a standard that measures a team's academic progress by assigning points to each individual student-athlete for eligibility and retention/graduation.

In Division II, student-athletes must complete 24 hours of degree credit each academic year to remain eligible for competition. At least 18 of those hours must be earned between the start of fall classes and spring commencement at a student-athlete's institution (six hours may be earned in the summer). All Division II student-athletes also must earn at least six credit hours each full-time term to be eligible for the following term.

In addition, Division II student-athletes must earn a 1.8 cumulative grade-point average after earning 24 hours, a 1.9 cumulative grade-point average after earning 48 hours and a 2.0 cumulative grade-point average after earning 72 hours to remain eligible. Student-athletes are given 10 semesters of full-time enrollment in which to use their four seasons of competition, provided they maintain academic eligibility.

Division II student-athletes must complete their four seasons of competition within the first 10 semesters or 15 quarters of full-time enrollment.

While there are no minimum national standards for establishing or maintaining eligibility in Division III, student-athletes in that division must be in good academic standing and make satisfactory progress toward a degree as determined by the institution.

Division III student-athletes must be enrolled in at least 12 semester or quarter hours, regardless of an institution's own definition of "full time."

Institutions in all divisions must determine and certify the academic eligibility of each student-athlete who represents the school on the field of play. Institutions are responsible for withholding academically ineligible student-athletes from competition.

Waivers are available for many of these rules, including progress-toward-degree standards. Student-athletes who are declared academically ineligible must use the student-athlete reinstatement process to be restored to competition.

Credit: Reprinted with the permission of the National Collegiate Athletic Association

Make sure you are prepared and know what you are getting into before you commit to a specific program.

You know yourself best, so weigh the course load at each university, including their different academic programs, and figure out what you feel you can handle while playing baseball.

Don't fall into the thought process that playing a sport in college will take away from your studies and give you a greater chance of failure.

When I was in college, playing a sport kept me more regimented because I was forced to do mandatory study hall freshman year. When I knew our team had an upcoming road trip, I was forced to do projects a week in advance. This is how I learned to time manage better.

As an athlete you have to prepare in advance, and procrastination isn't an option.

A student who is a non-athlete has all the time in the world to finish that project and can allow distractions and procrastination to creep in. Your schedule is regimented and you must stick by it if you want to succeed in both baseball and schoolwork.

There was a boy I grew up playing against, a lefty pitcher who topped out at 92 mph during his junior year of high school. He had trouble maintaining grades in high school and did not get many opportunities from colleges. He went from high school straight to a Division III program and soon failed out. No one else was interested in his potential and his million-dollar arm.

> # Tip!
> Applying yourself to the point of success
> is honorable. I can't stress the pertinence of
> good grades enough; even if you have to get a
> tutor for every single class in your schedule, do it.

CHAPTER 4
PRIVATE INSTRUCTION
AND RED FLAGS

Distrust and caution are the parents of security.
—Benjamin Franklin

P rivate baseball lessons can be beneficial, but they can also be harmful if you don't choose your instructor wisely. If your doctor diagnosed you with some life-threatening disease and said the treatments will now cost "X" or you will die in six months, would you just say, "Okay, you got it! Let's do it!," or would you go for a second or third opinion before making a decision? Although choosing a baseball instructor isn't a life-or-death decision, it can have a huge impact on a player's career.

There are many pretenders in the baseball-lesson industry. Baseball instructors often have résumés, which include what they *say* they have done during their playing and/or coaching careers. But they have no proof. And if they have no proof, then maybe Dad is more qualified than the instructor you are paying. Do your research and find out. If you cannot verify what's on the résumé, that may be a red flag for you to move forward cautiously. The Internet is a valuable tool to research anyone at anytime. If you find nothing at all . . . potential red flag! Also check on the players that instructor trains and their successes. Don't be afraid to consult with those players directly to learn more specifics. Do the clients travel long distances for this instructor? Do scouts, agencies, or coaches recommend players to train with this instructor? Is his clientele mostly 10-year-olds who are learning the game or mostly advanced-level players?

Another red flag is when an instructor says, "I have figured it all out. This *is* definitely the correct way. My philosophy works and is the greatest. You must buy in." If you hear anything along those lines, you *must* proceed with caution. It's quite possible the person saying this may be on to something, but he also may not be. The baseball industry evolves, as does its instruction. Take a look back at pitchers from the 1960s. Do you notice their similar windups and all the leg kicks? Why don't we see the same style today? Because advancements in biomechanics have helped pitchers to develop more efficient motions that reduce injuries.

Instructors mostly teach based on their past experience as players or coaches, or what they learned at a coaches' convention. But instructors should also be open to trying new techniques and most importantly should be able to prove the validity of what they teach.

Coaches also need to consider physical differences and adapt their techniques accordingly. Here's one example. If Player B has two inches less on his reach than Player A and they are both roughly the same height, then Player A has an ever so slight advantage as a hitter simply because longer arms allow a batter to extend longer through the zone to allow for maximum room for error to occur. When the barrel of the bat matches the plane the ball is traveling on it increases your chances of hitting the ball on the barrel of the bat consistently pre-contact and post-contact. Someone with longer arms can hold that plane longer than someone with shorter arms, thus proving the advantage to

Upon getting into the hitting zone, before barrel gets to the plane and up until point of contact on the plane, the bat angle is pretty much equal for both Player A (Mike Just on left) and Player B (Connor Kolich on right). *Photo courtesy of Mike Just.*

the player with longer arms in this case. However, the start of the plane would be an equal playing field for both players, as you can see in the diagram below.

Though the plane of the zone is also equal for Player A and Player B, through its full extension point there's a slight advantage to Player A. So if Player A and Player B are fooled on a pitch and both catch the ball completely out in front of the plate, Player B may "cap" it off the end, while Player A may still hit the barrel of the bat, assuming both players know how to maximize their extension by holding the plane and pushing all the way through the hitting zone.

Both players have maximized their extension through contact and before the wrists turn over and the finish is complete. Notice the extra few inches Player A has due to his extra two inches of reach; in the event he is way out front, he can still potentially keep the at-bat alive. *Photo courtesy of Mike Just.*

Another advantage Player A has with a longer reach is on the low strike. He can create an angle on the low pitch that exposes more of the bat's surface area to the ball since his arms are longer and allow his reach to get down lower in the zone without compromising his eye level.

Since Player B is a player I happen to train, I stress the importance of his points of contact and zone coverage due to him having an average reach for his body type. A player born with longer arms has an ever so slight potential advantage, and now you know why. We are talking just inches of difference on a reach, but as you know, baseball is a game of inches.

It's hard to see from the picture angle, but Player A's bat angle has 5 degrees less angle drop on the low strike than player B, while the surface area angle of the bat is still being fully maximized. Notice in the picture above that Player A can get his hands below the hip line while the left arm is locked out (meaning he cannot create a bat angle that's any flatter unless he drops his back knee down more). However if his back knee drops beyond 90 degrees instead of transferring laterally, then his eye level drops, thus decreasing the chance he will square up the baseball on a consistent basis in that location due to increased head and eye movement. Notice Player B has to keep his hands at his hip line and cannot go any lower because his left arm is already locked out at that point. If he goes any lower he will have to drop his barrel and lose surface area or drop his back knee down and compromise some power in order to attempt to hit a line drive. It's equally as important to match the angle of the ball coming in. Sometimes a player will have to have his barrel with an angle more below the hands than that depicted in the photos above in an instance where a curve ball is dropping low in the hitting zone so the player can have a preferred outgoing launch angle between a 15 and 25 degree trajectory. In the example above, we are assuming the ball is a straight fastball. *Photos courtesy of Mike Just.*

> ## Tip!
> Launch angle is the elevation of the ball leaving the bat post-contact. Some stronger MLB hitters can make a 30-35 degree launch angle carry out of the park with sheer strength and immense backspin. For other players, a 30-35 degree angle may become a fly out so the targeted launch angle falls between a 15 and 25 degree trajectory for most high school, college, and pro players desiring gap to gap line drives.

There are many different roads that can lead to success, but there are certain teaching methods that will stand out and have long-lasting positive results. Ask yourself this important question: Does your instructor prove to you *why*? When he teaches, does he teach because somewhere down the line someone taught him and therefore he's stamping that idea as fact without evidence to back it up? Or is he teaching you something that he can prove true with specific components of mathematics and physics? Rather than just saying, "Do this because I'm a former pro player and I said so," instructors should be able to communicate on a higher level. For example, 2+2=4. It's one thing to know it's correct, but it's another thing to be able to communicate why it's correct. Coaches need to recognize that no one style is best for every player. Look at the Japanese hitting style. It couldn't be more different from the typical US approach, but it worked well for Hideki Matsui and Ichiro Suzuki and many other Japanese players. Watch Japan in the Little League World Series and you will see the differences in their style of play.

Mike Just working with client Peter Chugranis. *Photos courtesy of Mike Just.*

Variables such as size of the player, bat speed, strength, and elasticity of muscles (affecting a player's ability to maximize whip to produce bat speed and maximum extension) all play a factor. I may or may not train my power guy to hit the exact same way as my leadoff hitter. My power guy's priority is to manufacture RBIs, so I may stress the importance of bottom hand and leverage through the zone to optimize a 25-30 degree launch angle. With my leadoff hitter, on the other hand, I may focus on a more top-hand, short-compact approach, to optimize a 15-25 degree launch angle. I say "may" because good coaches need to treat each player as an individual and adapt their teaching methods accordingly.

There *are* right and wrong ways to do things. For example, batting stances are partly a matter of preference, but the stance cannot impede the rhythm and timing of the load. Some instructors use a "cookie-cutter" approach and insist that all their players use the same stance, right down to bat positioning and the front-foot stride (which if you study your Big Leaguers, there are three commonly used stride variations, not only one). But a good instructor should understand that different stances work for different players, while still being able to spot and correct a stance that will negatively affect a player's production. A load is when you "walk" your hands, arms, and some of your lower half back to an optimum launch position to generate what's known as a negative to positive. Think of a sling shot or bow and arrow effect.

Coaches may be experts on one particular style of hitting, but they need to be flexible. Coaches who are big weight shift teachers need to understand that batters could have trouble recognizing off-speed pitches. Coaches who are big rotational teachers need to realize there could be problems maximizing power and extension to the opposite field, and they need to understand proper energy transfer and distribution based on specific points of contact. Picking out the key components from many different styles to create a niche that works can be beneficial, but only if the coach truly understands what he is teaching and why he is teaching it, and is willing to put his pride aside and always be a sponge soaking up new information.

The higher level you play, the more intricacies you learn. When I played in high school, if you asked me point blank, "Mike, do you know the game of baseball?," my response would have been, "100 percent! I get it and completely understand it." Then when I was in college, if you asked me again, "Mike, do you know the game?," my response would have been, "Well I thought I did in high school, but there's a lot more involved than I thought at this college level."

Then when I was actually asked after I had former big-league managers as my managers in the Atlantic League, "Mike, do you know the game?," my response was indeed, "Actually, no. Not

From left to right: Joe Klein (former Atlantic League commissioner), Butch Hobson, Mike Just. *Photo courtesy of Joe Klein.*

as much as I thought I did. There's so much to it that only one achieving this level of expertise can truly understand and appreciate the amount involved." An instructor doesn't know what he flat out doesn't learn through experience and the reality of it is that he may never find out or realize his inexperience so he communicates as if he knows.

When I played under Butch Hobson, who formerly managed the Red Sox, he used to hold a meeting before every opposing series in the clubhouse. He would go down the opposing lineup and he would ask us, "Who played with this player? What are his strengths and what are his weaknesses?" Even if he knew a player well, he wanted all of us to know and be on the same page and he wanted the latest on that player. We would then create mental scouting reports and charts on each individual player. From there, Butch would formulate how the pitchers were to attack a particular hitter, sometimes down to the count and where we would position ourselves in every circumstance. That's a small segment of what you get from a major-league manager.

Unless you have been to a level at which you can understand and appreciate the importance and purpose of every pitch, you may not know what you don't know. No book that is read, no coaches conference attended, can replace hands-on experience. Some instructors do not have experience playing at a high level, but are excellent communicators of the game because they had great coaches or baseball mentors. There are former major leaguers who had terrible communication skills and can't get a player to hit a lick.

One coach used to say literally every time a hitter hit a groundball or popup, "Just feel it. Ya gotta feel it."

What does that even mean? Just feel what? What are we feeling here?

It's important to understand that just because a player played in pro ball and may have even performed well at that level, he doesn't necessarily have the gift of communication skills and the ability to establish a connection with his students.

What you are looking for as a parent or player is what I call "the perfect combo"—experience and communication skills, while avoiding the aforementioned red flags.

There are other factors that you should most definitely consider. What character does this instructor have? When you sign up for lessons, you are signing up for more than just baseball.

An athlete will put a former pro player on a pedestal. You are setting your child up with a role model. If your instructor chews tobacco, smokes, curses, or discusses lewd acts as if it's everyday normal conversation, then you have a red-flag situation. Good instructors also support their clients by attending some of their games or at least asking for the results via texts from the parents or the player.

Character is vital when choosing your instructor. You don't want your son to learn to hit a baseball better at the expense of his lifestyle and character.

Remember that a player will often be more likely to listen to the instructor than the parent, even if the same exact thing is being said. The instructor should never replace the parent, but if he works together with the parent, great things can happen. Choose an instructor wisely, because he can either have a positive or negative influence on character while bettering or worsening your career.

CHAPTER 5
GOAL SETTING AND VALUES

Strive not to be a success but rather to be of value.
—Albert Einstein

Goals Can Create Focus and Motivation

Goal setting helps develop realistic expectations for baseball as well as academics, and nurtures vision and the value of perspective. Players need to set goals for how they are going to represent themselves both on and off the field.

Players should develop a grid for decision-making, which will equip them to make better decisions, from matters like integrity and performance-enhancing drugs, to how to be a team player.

If you have never set goals, then you have no idea how far your talent can take you.

I didn't realize how true this was until I spoke to an Oakland A's scout before my 2007 season. I wanted a firm answer on what I needed to do to get an affiliated contract and I couldn't get a straight answer.

I said, "The Northern League has a ton of triple-A guys in it, correct? So if I hit .300 in that league then would that be impressive?"

He replied, "Absolutely Mike!"

"So what on-base percentage would suffice because we are living this Billy Beane Moneyball thing right now and I'm good to go with the walk to strikeout ratio. What do I need for OBP?"

He answers, ".380 would be the minimum to be impressive."

I reply, "Okay done! What else."

He chuckles, "Some doubles, stolen bases . . ."

"How's 20 of each? Good plan?"

He chuckles again, "Yes, Mike, why not!"

I proceed to tell him I will make no more than five errors all season, and just for kicks I will hit at least .333 to be safe.

He didn't believe me.

I closed with, "I will call you in 100 games." I sat down, took out a sheet of paper, set my goals, and reflected on them every night before I went to sleep.

A few nights before our first game I was driving to the town of Fargo where our home field was located, and I was eating at a Red Lobster when I saw on the television that Jerry Falwell Sr. had passed away. He was a large influence in my life, not only because he was the president and founder of my alma mater Liberty University, but also because he was someone I admired for standing up for what he believed in regardless of what other people thought.

My grandfather (Anthony Just Sr.), who was the mayor of Secaucus, New Jersey, throughout the 1990s and a sergeant in the Korean War, had morals and ideology similar to President Falwell. His mayoral campaign theme song was "My Way" by Frank Sinatra.

With the passing of President Falwell, I had decided to take out that sheet of paper with my goals on it and dedicate that season to him.

That season I hit .336, with 24 doubles, 20 stolen bases, 44 walks, 37 strikeouts, exactly five errors, and an OBP of .420.

A friendly meeting of two parties joining together to work as a team between Republican Mayor of NYC Rudy Giuliani and Democratic Mayor of Secaucus, NJ, Anthony Just. *Photo Courtesy of Mayor Giuliani's Office NYC.*

Brittany Just, Jerry Falwell Sr., and Mike Just. *Photo courtesy of Clayton Young.*

Time Management Chart

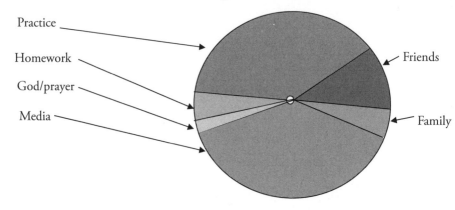

I heard that Oakland was highly considering me, but still dragging its feet. However, by the end of that year the Houston Astros locked me up. That's the power of goal setting!

Make sure you set your goals and chase your dreams!

Anything is possible! I am a man of faith and I trusted in that faith for guidance along the way. Unfortunately, I also lost my grandfather in December 2007 after that season ended. Two great men of faith and leadership in my life passed away in the same year.

Setting proper goals starts with the vision mapping process or wheel of life balance.

The example in the wheel above is based on roughly eight hours of time, from when school lets out to when the player goes to sleep. It's a random example from one of my high school players and should not be taken as the standard. The wheel allows a player to see clearly what and where he spends most of his time after school.

Time is our most important resource and must be managed properly. If the player above examines the wheel, he will realize how significantly out of balance his time is. He can devote more time to areas that will be the most beneficial and shave off some hours from other less important categories.

A wheel out of balance cannot roll properly. Balance is the key and a player needs to make sure he isn't spending too much time on any one task. In the wheel above, media seems to consume most of the player's time. That's something that needs to be altered in order for this player to accomplish more important tasks that will help him achieve his goals.

Most players' wheel of life diagrams will include the following categories: practice (whether that be your main sport, any other sports, and/or an instrument or anything that involves your time to practice), homework, media (TV, Internet, video games, social media), friends (time spent after school), and family. You may have other categories that are specific to you, such as religious or community activities. Feel free to add to or subtract from the ones listed and try to create a more balanced wheel for yourself. After the wheel is accurately drawn up, a player can not only set goals, but can start to accomplish those goals by mapping out the process to start conquering those challenges.

Taking Chances—Don't Be Afraid to Fail

Baseball is a game of failure. How do you enjoy a game where you fail more than you succeed? There's no other game in which you can fail 7 out of 10 times and be considered a good player. The challenge is all mental.

Your personality affects your mentality, which can affect your production on the field. Someone who is extremely sensitive and extroverted may have a harder time restraining himself and keeping his composure in times of failure, while introverts with high levels of intuition may be better at handling setbacks.

However, regardless of your personality, baseball is its own acquired personality. One must learn to adapt to play the game of baseball successfully as you climb the ladder. Even-keeled is the baseball player personality trait of choice. Don't let your highs get too high or your lows get too low.

A few major leaguers still struggle with this. Some veterans make an out or an error and shrug it off, yet learn from it and move on, while some players may smash their bat into the bat rack or throw the cooler.

If a player hits a home run in the third inning, but his team loses a nail-biter, and he's all smiles at the end of the game anyway, he does not fully understand what it means to be even-keeled. Out of respect for his teammates, he should not have let his highs get that high. If his parents are also all smiles and are overly cheerful after the loss, it is disrespectful to the coach and the other team-mates. This works the other way, too. If you just won the nail-biter and you were 0-for-4 with an error in the field, you should be in a celebratory mood because your team just won the game.

Sulking will put a damper on the victory and is selfish. If your parents are reprimanding you in front of other players because of your poor performance regardless of the victory, then they are acting selfishly as well.

No one enjoys playing with those that let their highs get too high and their lows get too low. A game-winning hit is a whole different story of course. This is applicable to life off the field as well.

What happens down the road if your budget is running low and you receive a bill in the mail saying the tax assessor assessed your house for $2000 more, just as your five-year-old is pulling your shirt to play catch with you? Do you sulk and get angry at your child in the moment and purposely avoid him and worry over the issue, or do you stay even-keeled, put the bill down, and think to yourself, "This can wait. I will tackle this first thing tomorrow, but for the moment my son will have my full attention."

What people call "even-keeled" on the baseball field is sometimes called "maturity" out in the real world.

Tip!
The clearer your mind is, the more you can see.

When your mind is clouded with frustration and anger, you don't make wise decisions. This game is all about taking chances and climbing the ladder to play against better competition. Without a solid and clear mentality to match your ability, you will end up being nothing more than wasted talent.

If you fear you are weak mentally, then you are normal. I acquired mental toughness due to years of training and experiences, and every day it is still a struggle.

During my career I watched former major leaguers and how they carried themselves on the field, in the dugouts, in the clubhouse,

Tip!
Watch, learn, and open your heart
and mind to advice (especially if you are
told something more than once) and avoid
rebuttals with excuses. Focus on what is important.
Rather than sulking, think positively and
confidently and behave in a way that won't
hinder your progress.

and on road trips, and I learned from the good ones and the bad ones. I learned who I did and didn't want to emulate and why.

Take chances, make wise decisions, and take leaps of faith, trusting in your mentors and your own strong mental stability every step of the way.

Performance-Enhancing Drugs

PEDs are rampant throughout our country and other countries as well. There are many MLB players who are from the Dominican Republic, Venezuela, and other countries in Latin America or South America. The way of life in these countries is different from life in the United States. First, a majority of the children from these countries play baseball—and play it well. In the Dominican Republic baseball is a way to a better life. Players are often willing to sacrifice many things to achieve their dream to play baseball in America. Scouts have created baseball schools in the Dominican Republic and Venezuela to groom players from the ground up.

Young players from these areas are happy to even own a glove, while well-to-do American players might own three different color gloves to match their socks. Most players from these countries are not in a strong position to negotiate.

College is not an option for most of them, either. They usually need to work to help provide for their families, and baseball is a realistic means for them to do that. Here in the United States, athletes have the luxury of a potential agent, and fallback options like college and other job opportunities.

Therefore, when a Dominican or Venezuelan player is offered steroids and told these drugs may help him live a life of stardom and help provide for his family for a lifetime if he can just add five more MPH to his fastball, he may be willing to risk it all for a better chance at success . . . even when there's a chance he may get caught, ruin his reputation, and potentially die earlier in life. The majority of the players from these nations who use steroids aren't thinking big picture or long term. There have been many high-profile US-born steroid abusers as well due to the pressures to make it big. Regardless of where the players hail from, they use steroids because of the intense pressure to get to or stay in the major leagues, or because they think it gives them a mental edge. Whatever rationale players use, performance-enhancing drugs (PEDs) are illegal and harmful, and the consequences of getting caught are only becoming more severe.

According to the National Institute on Drug Abuse (https://www.drugabuse.gov/publications/research-reports/anabolic-steroid-abuse/what-are-health-consequences-steroid-abuse), here are the consequences of using performance-enhancing drugs:

- Extreme fines to career ending consequences.
- Defame your name.
- Effects to the human body: jaw bone enlarges, acne and cysts, oily scalp, jaundice, HIV/AIDS, hepatitis, breast development, heart attacks, liver tumors and cancer, infertility, shrinking of testicles, male pattern baldness, tendon ruptures.
- Psychological effects: rage/aggression, mania, delusions.
- Earlier death.

Not all performance-enhancing drugs are steroids. Players also use "greenies" to try to get an extra edge.

The aforementioned steroids are mostly used for muscle building, but greenies are stimulants that directly affect the player's nerves. Players who have taken them report they make the athlete super alert and decrease muscle fatigue over the course of the season. Players who use them rarely tire out. Cocaine was the drug of choice in the 1970s and 1980s. Greenies were around then too, but are now much more prevalent.

There's no advantage to a player becoming overly jittery when he's trying to relax and hit a 95-mph fastball. However, if you *think* you have an edge from, let's say, drinking an abundance of water, then you have an edge . . . baseball is that mental.

Some players also take Adderall. They get a family member or friend who is a doctor to diagnose them with attention-deficit disorder (ADD), and then they are legally able to take the focus pills. Before you know it, they are hitting 100 points higher because they are so locked in. Greenies are still abundant in baseball clubhouses. MLB will continue to crack down on the use of these stimulants as well as PEDs.

If you are considering using a PED or stimulant, block the temptation and weigh the quality of your life and your future. Think of your family, reputation, and health. It is not worth the risk.

Tip!
You can have all the success in the world,
but money doesn't buy you happiness.

Even if you think you'll never get caught, and you're foolish enough to think PEDs won't permanently damage your health or lead to an early death, don't conceal a lie the rest of your life. Achieve success the right way, which is more rewarding and something to be proud of.

Be a Team Player

Every franchise has its share of selfish players and team players.

Team players work together, encourage and uplift others, play hard to win, and respect their teammates, their opponents, and the game.

When I played for Butch Hobson, I discovered that he was careful to ask players who had played with me about my character as he considered making a trade for me. He asked:

"What is Mike like?"

"Is he a solid clubhouse guy?"

"Would he be an asset to our organization or a liability?"

"Does he have self-control?"

Fortunately for me, I met all of the criteria from the perspective of a catcher with whom I played in 2007 in the Northern League. The solid clubhouse guy criteria may or may not have had something to do with my clubhouse dance moves in boxers to "Boogie Shoes" or rather singing Lionel Richie in the showers with our center fielder while the rest of the team sang backup. (I'll leave his name out so he can maintain his manliness.)

Butch then made the move to acquire me.

When I was there, I heard him ask similar questions about other players, and when Butch didn't like the answer, Butch didn't care who you were, he was no longer interested. He did not want to disrupt the camaraderie he had worked so hard to build just to acquire a selfish stud.

Scouts and coaches alike enjoy an atmosphere where a team gels together. Nobody enjoys the selfish player and nobody wants one on their team. The player who is a prima donna and parents who act the same ruin the atmosphere for everyone involved. The parents mainly fill the player's head with false hope, and the selfish player's perception is not the same as the rest of his teammates or his coach.

No scout, and I repeat *no scout*, wants to sign this player.

A scout may do so anyway because of the player's extreme ability, but the organization will pay the price down the line. Can a player's selfish ways transfer onto the field negatively? Absolutely! For example, if you are down a run and you personally are 0-for-3 on the day and you are up for the fourth time with nobody out, and it's the last inning and there is a man on second base, your job as a hitter is to get that runner to third any way you can. You can bunt him over or hit a groundball to the right side. You can attempt to stay inside the ball at all costs to advance that runner by giving yourself up. These are options that are best for your team, but could hurt your personal batting average.

A selfish player doesn't even consider the options. He sees a pitch to drive and he swings hard regardless of the outcome, hoping for a hit to tie the game and boost his average. Sometimes that player will prevail, but the odds are against him, because baseball is a game of failure. If he plays the odds and gets that runner to third with one out, chances are that runner will score time and time again. It's not guaranteed but the odds fall in your team's favor.

Tip!

I've even played with guys who were 0-for-3 on the day, got the bunt sign, and purposely tried to foul one off or take the pitch altogether just so they could get to two strikes in order to have a swinging chance to get a hit. The coach won't stand for those antics long and he'll catch on sooner rather than later.

A scout once had a high-ranking recruit who he was supposed to draft, but didn't because of his selfish ways. The player was a solid hitter and was ranked nationally. The scout went to his games and he was crushing the ball. He was having consistent games of 3-for-3s and 3-for-4s. The scout knew he could hit, but wanted to see how he carried himself during a time of failure. Does he still run hard for his team or does he pack it in?

The next game the player popped out three times and the third time he jogged to first, barely reaching first base, threw his helmet, and walked out to his position. The scout put an "X" through his name on a list of top recruits, packed up his things, and left.

CHAPTER 6
THE MENTAL SIDE
OF THE GAME

Half the game is 90 percent mental.
—Yogi Berra

M any players can hit a baseball, but not many can handle the mental game.

Former 11-year big leaguer Michael Tucker told me, "When I'm up at the plate, I know I'm better than the pitcher. If I'm 0-for-4, he didn't beat me or is any better than me. He just got lucky I didn't have it today." You may mistake Tucker's confidence for cockiness; however, in this game you have to have an edge.

Tip!
If there is any doubt in your mind that you
might not succeed before you get into the box,
you have already failed.

One day, Tucker noticed I wasn't myself, so he approached me and gave me that helpful advice when I needed it the most.

I went through a period where I was lining out once, sometimes twice a game. Two teammates consulted me and both had similar advice. One asked me, "What are you thinking about when you're at the plate?" I told him, "I'm thinking that I know I'm going to make solid contact but it's going to go right at someone." He said, "Do you realize what you are doing? You are confident that you are going to hit the ball, but you are also willing yourself to hit the ball at everyone out there!" I told him he was crazy since our minds don't have the power to change a result like that!

Or do they?

He proceeded to say, "I want you to try this in today's game. Go up in the box knowing you're going to hit the ball, no matter how you get the job done, you don't hit it at anyone." I had nothing to lose so I gave it a shot. That night I was 2-for-4 with an RBI, but let me tell you that it was the hardest I've hit the ball all four at-bats all season long.

I kept that mentality and ended up hitting over .400 for that week in pro ball. I still hit the ball to people, but I got my share of hits as well. This helped me surpass a huge mental barrier. If my mental preparation and positive outlook is there, I can achieve more than my physical talent alone will allow me to. This was a high bar to hurdle, but it got me to think properly when I stepped in the batter's box.

There are all sorts of mental adjustments you can make and mental toughness hurdles to overcome in baseball. Prepare your mind and think positively. You have to believe you can do it and overcome anything.

Your mind is powerful.

It may be a mindset that is simplistic, like what you are going to do with the ball if it is hit to you. Maybe it's what to do when you are on the bases. Whether you are on the field, in the dugout, in the car, or at home, always envision yourself succeeding and always think positive about yourself and your abilities.

Strive to be better.

Practice smart.

It's more about the quality than the quantity. Sometimes both are necessary and you will know when that's the case. Always try as hard as you can and whether you succeed or you fail, be happy with the results because the effort and preparation is where you find your pride and contentment. Don't fall into the trap of being solely result-oriented. If so, baseball will let you down because it is a game of failure. Set your personal "bar" based on the effort you put forth and the confidence you acquire, but not entirely in the results. The game will be more enjoyable and that mental maturity will suit you well as you progress up the baseball ladder. If easier for you to determine, keep two stat sheets—one of the actual stats, and one of quality at bats. Some characteristics of a quality at bat include: the ability to go deep in counts when the time calls for it, hard hit balls right at someone, going the other way to move the runner over, and many more scenarios.

If a negative thought enters your mind, cancel it or, better yet, change the channel on that thought to something positive.

You can hit any pitcher, steal any base, make any play, and when you don't, you will do awesome next time. That's thinking like a pro.

Some coaches will tell you to not worry about mechanics, and if you think positive enough then mechanics will work themselves out. Some coaches rely solely upon the mechanics to attempt to succeed. The best solution is about a 50/50 split of both mechanics and mental confidence. It does a player no good to focus on positive thoughts and have a long bat path to the ball so he cannot physically hit it even if his confidence is sky high. It also does a player no good to drill a solid bat path and not think he can actually succeed. A safe mix of both realms (physical mechanics and mental confidence) will allow a player to optimize his performance.

The Just Experience

In Extra Bases Appendix E, Mike Just's Story, there is a short story from my career about discovering a more personal mental toughness scenario.

As part of my mental preparation, I used to close my eyes and visualize catching all sorts of groundballs. I used to envision the field and the layout, the divots, even the consistency of the clay, sand, or crushed brick ground. I used to envision good throws and bad throws while receiving double plays and how I would still make the play happen regardless. I would prepare to react to anything and think about how nothing would get by me. At home as a young kid I would bounce a tennis ball off the brick fireplace while watching TV. I would use my peripheral vision to catch the ball while watching episodes after episodes of TV. I

Photo courtesy of Les Schofer and Liberty University.

used to be able to pick balls with ease in the games due to this routine.

I attribute a large part of my fielding success to my mental preparation too. I only had 10 errors in four years of Division I baseball at Liberty University as a second baseman. That was the best in the conference and state.

Challenge yourself mentally and open up a whole new path of success for yourself and your career.

CHAPTER 7
THE NEXT LEVEL

*Perfection is not attainable, but if we chase perfection
we can catch excellence.*
—Vince Lombardi

Excellence is a worthy pursuit for all players. If you have done your best, then you can play and live with no regrets. Striving for excellence is about heart and attitude as well as the physical aspects of the game.

How do you become the best you can be?

What path will get you to the next level?

What micro goals are difference makers for achieving the overall goal of getting to the pros, playing in college, playing varsity, or making the elite travel team?

Every player needs to challenge himself. However, identifying the right targets is also essential. So often we become overly focused on our peer competition, those whom we play with regularly, and are constantly measuring ourselves against them. At some level that is relevant. But what if you play with a group of underachievers or what if you play with an extremely talented group of athletes in a highly competitive league? Having an objective standard will help define your targets and cast the right vision of what could be.

So what does it take to get to the next level?

We begin with looking at the profile of each position, then move to scouts, and finally to understanding the position you play.

How Do I Stack Up Against the Profile?

In baseball there are certain desired abilities for each position, and these are known as the *tools of the trade*. Every organization and team is different, so there will be some deviations, but proficiencies in fielding, arm strength, hitting, power, and speed are always among the tools that are rated.

The chart below is a general overview. It has each position with the most important tool listed directly beneath it and then moving in descending order to the bottom. For example, fielding is the most valuable skill for catchers and speed is the area that is de-emphasized. Also note that pitchers are not included because they are judged by a different paradigm. Pitchers will be discussed separately.

Position Players' Five Tools in Order of Importance

LEFT FIELD	CENTER FIELD	RIGHT FIELD	FIRST BASE	SECOND BASE	SHORT-STOP	THIRD BASE	CATCHER
Hitting	Speed	Hitting	Hitting	Hitting	Fielding	Hitting	Fielding
Power	Fielding	Arm	Power	Fielding	Hitting	Power	Arm
Fielding	Hitting	Power	Fielding	Speed	Arm	Fielding	Hitting
Speed	Arm	Fielding	Arm	Power	Speed	Arm	Power
Arm	Power	Speed	Speed	Arm	Power	Speed	Speed

First basemen and third basemen tools are generally universal throughout organizations. Other positions can vary some depending on the organizational needs.

This chart can help you to rank your baseball abilities per position in order of importance. After you rate yourself, then compare your rankings to the chart's priorities and the position you play. This will identify areas where you need to focus for improvement. This chart is not exact because each organization has different criteria, but it is as close to the middle ground as possible.

What Do Scouts Look For?

Scouts approach the game from a variety of perspectives. The old school scouts rely on their "gut" and factors like sound—the sound of the bat or the sound of the ball hitting the catcher's glove. They will often say they do not have to see it, just hear it. Some scouts look for sheer athleticism, potential, and projection down the road. Some are purely statistical and rely only on the numbers. Most use something from all of these approaches.

To have someone take a personal interest in you as a player can be so rewarding. Furthermore, to be scouted by colleges or pros can give you quite a rush; it is such a compliment. After all, someone thinks you are talented. An outsider's attention can sometimes confuse parents and players alike because not all may have your best intentions in mind when they are pursuing you. The more you know about scouting, the more equipped you will be to take advantage of the right opportunities.

There is a pecking order in the scouting world. Some have influence and others have no influence. Knowing what kind of scout you are talking to will help you interpret the merits of the attention being given.

The general scouting manager is in the top position. In order of importance, the basic outline for the pyramid of scouting is below:

- General Scouting Manager
- Scouting Director
- Assistant Scouting Director
- Special Assignment Scout
- National Cross-Checker Scout
- Regional Scout

- Area Scout
- Part-Time Scout
- Bird Dog Scout

Some people will try to pass themselves off as a scout, when they are not. A "bird dog" scout is technically part of the scouting pyramid but is only a volunteer. He hopes that he has a player that the part-time or area scout would like. More often than not, the bird dog scout has no direct clout with an organization. Almost anyone with a network in the industry could classify themselves as a bird dog.

If approached by someone, do not hesitate to ask what kind of scout they are then research their response thereafter as well for validation. An area scout or above has significant influence on the pyramid, and getting on their radar can create opportunities.

Tools of Hitting and Pitching

Scouts rate positions. This means the player is evaluated based upon their ability to execute the five tools in the specific position they are playing when scouted. In the context of the position, a player is rated on a 20/80 scale, or 2 to 8. This rating scale is designed to project whether or not a player can perform at the pro level. The five tools being rated are:

1. Hitting
2. Hitting for Power
3. Fielding
4. Arm Strength
5. Speed

On the 2 to 8 scale, scouts are looking for players with a minimum average of 5 or better as a total for all the categories. Scoring a 5 or better implies the player projects as average major-league potential. Pitchers are evaluated in different categories, which will be discussed in the next section.

Tool #1: Hitting

Hitting is important, but its significance fluctuates depending upon the position and the MLB team. However, there are some general rules of thumb. Outfielders need to hit well along with the corner infielders (first and third) and the shortstop somewhat. Second basemen use to have some leeway in this category, but this seems to be changing and the hitting expectations for them are also higher than in the past. For catchers, it depends upon the team. Some prefer a strong defensive catcher over their offensive production, while other teams prefer the opposite.

Obviously, to excel at both is a plus. If you are an effective switch-hitter, then you have an advantage. All around, hitting is becoming more and more essential as a tool and is usually the tool that is the most appealing.

Tool #2: Hitting for Power

The higher the exit velocity of the ball off the bat, the more power you have. This in turn produces more hits, assuming you have an eye for the strike zone.

Technicalities and talent aside, baseball is a business and home runs are good for business.

> ## *The Just Experience*
> Fans love the longball. Years ago the home-run race between Mark McGwire and Sammy Sosa made headlines, and then again with Barry Bonds chasing the all-time mark. Everyone was watching and talking about baseball when these record breakers were coming up to bat. Ratings were up, which means revenues and profits increased. It adds excitement to the game. The MLB even has dedicated events like the Home Run Derby.

The bottom line is: Hitting for power matters.

Corner players, corner outfielders, and most catchers need to swing for power. Shortstops and second basemen do not have quite the expectation placed on them for power hitting as other positions.

However, when players like Cal Ripken Jr., Nomar Garciaparra, Alex Rodriguez, and Derek Jeter came along, then some expectations can begin being redefined. They all established a new power standard for shortstops.

Tool #3: Fielding

Fielding is much more than catching the ball and throwing the runner out at first. Scouts are also looking for footwork and range.

How efficient and smooth is the player in approaching the ball?

Is he proactive and aggressive, yet under control?

Is he efficient with his footwork, meaning does it take him 12 steps to get to the ball as opposed to the necessary five or six?

How is his first step?

Does he cover a lot of ground? More specifically, is each particular step efficient, and does each serve a purpose while reducing the maximum amount of ground contact?

Is he lazy and/or uncertain about how to approach the ball?

Is he able to effectively field the ball with the understanding of where the ball goes next based upon the changing dynamics of a ball hit off the bat?

Does he take a strong shuffle (if in the infield) or crow-hop (if in the outfield) and follow his throw upon his release?

When a scout watches you field the ball, these are the kinds of questions he is trying to answer to also see if you're versatile as a player. Footwork and a sense of the game are vital, and the more a scout can envision you at multiple positions, the more your stock increases.

Shortstops have an advantage. College and pro scouts have a tendency to recruit shortstops knowing they are already capable of playing second, third, or even first base. Why not recruit the most athletic player in the infield multiple times to play every position in the infield if possible, rather than recruiting the first baseman that may just be pigeon-holed to first base?

Other tools such as power and defense can still make a corner infielder stand out. A player who currently doesn't have great footwork may still have projectable skills that can be improved and developed over time, and a scout will take that into consideration.

Tool #4: Arm Strength

Arm strength is critical at any position in today's game. A second baseman has to be able to play short or third in a pinch, which means even this position has to have good arm strength. A player has more value when he is adept at multiple positions. Versatility is vital!

Tip!

The above average big-league infielder throws the ball between 87 and 90 mph. You can build your arm strength by doing a long toss program and use resistance bands and light weights to strengthen your rotators.

Incorporating a long toss program into your regimen will increase your arm strength. See Extra Bases Appendix B for additional information.

Tool #5: Speed

Speed does not always refer to stolen bases. It is absolutely crucial for middle infielders and center fielders. Corner outfielders need speed as well, but it is more of a priority for center fielders. With regard to speed, scouts are thinking and asking themselves questions such as:

- How much ground does the player cover in the outfield, and how quickly?
- How much range—playing the position and backing up throws—does the player have in the infield?
- How well does he run bases?
- Does the player hustle and is hustle second nature?

The answer to these questions will impact how a player scores in the area of speed. A player can improve his speed with proper technique. Quickness can be increased doing various exercises. For instance, running sprints correctly promotes speed and endurance.

Efficiency is one way to improve your speed both on defense and offense. For example, how you run the bases matters, and there is an efficiency in baserunning that serious players need to incorporate into their game. Dipping the left shoulder down and angling the foot to hit the inside, front corner of the base allows for maximum speed and control when changing direction to round the bases. Pumping your arms from "chin to pocket" allows for proper stride length and maximum leg speed. Short pumps of the arms result in short, choppy steps with the feet. Long pendulum arm swings result in longer, slower strides.

Your body wants to keep a rhythm, so make sure that rhythm is productive. These techniques should be applied every time the bases are run regardless of who is watching and whether or not it is practice or game time.

Remember, not all pro players have all of the tools. These standards should be viewed as benchmarks, a way for you to set goals and to assess your own performance.

There are a number of talented athletes who never played at the next level because they had no vision for it and no one ever challenged them

Mike Just demonstrates a slightly forward lean with a "chin to pocket" arm motion and elbows fixed at 90 degrees. A small thing such as leaving gaps between fingers keeps the upper body loose. If fingers are touching, muscles in the forearms, biceps, and chest tighten and will not be as effective for explosiveness. *Photo courtesy of Mike Just.*

to consider it. These benchmarks help to cast a vision for improving your game while giving you a realistic context of expectations.

> ## Tip!
> In the scouting world it is often said:
> Just do everything good, or better yet,
> one thing great, and you will stand out.

Pitchers

Pitchers are evaluated on a completely different paradigm. It includes being rated on the six different tools listed and detailed below:

1. Fastball Velocity
2. Command
3. Pitch-ability
4. Arm Action/Arm Speed
5. Overall Athleticism
6. Deception

Pitching Tool #1: Fastball Velocity

Fastball velocity is a term used to indicate the speed of the ball out of the player's hand. There are many factors that can affect a pitcher's velocity, but the two most recognized by the industry are genetics and mechanics. Obviously there is not much to be done about genetics, but it is good to know that one's physical profile can impact this area.

Some players have the ability to create more whip with their arm based on certain muscles, elasticity, and explosiveness.

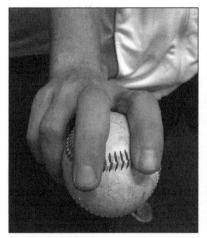

Former pro pitcher Ryan Page shows both sides of a four-seam fastball grip from a right-hander. A four-seam grip is the grip best used for maximum velocity because the four seams cut through the air upon its release. Some pitchers will spread their fingers a tad wider or keep them a tad closer or rotate to either side of the "horse-shoe." For the most accurate throw, the thumb should be almost directly underneath the baseball and may be positioned somewhat on the right side of the thumb if a righty and left for lefty. If the thumb slides up to the side of the baseball, the ball will have a tendency to move laterally. *Photo courtesy of Mike Just.*

Height (over six feet) usually helps to give a pitcher more leverage, which can help with both speed and power. Height also has been known to translate to less wear and tear on the body than for someone who is under six feet. This does not mean that all pitchers have to be six feet or above or that a pitcher who is taller will always be better. In general, the majority of pitchers have a tall, lanky build known as a "solid frame."

However, there is not a perfect physical profile, which is why you see some pitchers at 5'10" throwing 95 mph and some pitchers at 6'5" only throwing 80 mph and vice versa. There are a variety of body types at the major-league level.

Regarding mechanics, there are four specific parts that will affect the height of the pitch—weight distribution, separating the hands on time at the beginning of the motion, front arm pull, and extension at the end of the pitch. There are three body parts that will affect the pitch horizontally—placement of front foot, hip activation, and front arm pull.

An example of former pro pitcher Ryan Page's weight distribution, arm pull, and extension of a pitch upon delivery:

Ryan Page demonstrates a pitcher's delivery sequentially. *Photo courtesy of Lara DiNatale.*

> ## Tip!
> In order to maximize velocity, the pitcher must keep his weight back on his back leg until after the front foot hits the ground. This allows for more torque to be built up and for all the pitcher's power and momentum to remain together.

Pitching Tool #2: Command

Pitchers normally are graded first on their individual pitches, which will consist of a fastball, changeup, the best breaking pitch (curveball/slider), and/or the "out pitch," if they have one. An out pitch is defined as a pitch that is purposefully thrown in the dirt, but because the ball breaks so late the batter is deceived and baited into swinging. The pitch will start out appearing to be in the strike zone, yet by the time it reaches the plate, it will have fallen off track, down into the dirt where the hitter cannot actually make contact with it. This deception adds to the baseball IQ of the pitcher. "Out pitches" are generally curveballs, changeups, or splitters, depending upon which one you can command and throw the best.

The pitches mentioned will be graded individually and will receive two scores: one for velocity and the other for command. Note: Command is different than control. Control of a pitch is the ability to throw the pitch for a strike. Commanding a pitch requires a more advanced skill and is defined as delivering a pitch to a certain part of the strike zone. When a pitcher can fully understand how his body works within the pitching motion, he will be able to control each of his pitches successfully by adjusting certain mechanics to allow himself to command the strike zone consistently.

Pitching Tool #3: Pitch-ability

"Pitch-ability" is defined as knowing when to change pitches, speeds, and locations to keep hitters off balance and produce desired results. This is the mental aspect of the six tools that requires the utmost knowledge of baseball. For example, if a pitcher needs to get the batter to hit a groundball, he may choose to throw a two-seam fastball low in the strike zone to produce that desired result. If a right-handed batter has just pulled your four-seam fastball hard down the third base line, your next pitch should be a slower pitch on the outside of the plate to adjust the hitter's eye level and disrupt his timing, which can coax him to be out front and hit a soft popup somewhere or swing and miss altogether. However, if the hitter has a high baseball IQ and in the past has been known for correctly anticipating pitches, then perhaps you go back with the four-seam fastball inside in hopes of jamming him because he is thinking a slow pitch away. The strategy behind what pitches to throw and their location in pro ball is another game within the game, which makes each pitching decision all the more important.

Pitching Tool #4: Arm Action/Arm Speed

Arm action is the path the hand takes from the time the ball comes out of the glove to the release point. A pitcher's arm angle is often confused with his arm action. Arm angle is the biomechanic of each individual pitcher and should not be altered. Arm action, on the other hand, can be altered to ensure that the pitch looks smooth and to limit the amount of strain placed on the arm.

Arm action is also graded to determine the longevity of the pitcher. A pitcher with a smoother motion will generally last years longer than a pitcher who causes more strain on his arm due to poorer arm action. If you watch the majority of big leaguers throw in warm-ups, the ball is jumping out of their hand, popping the glove, and it looks effortless. This is due to excellent arm action and their ability to utilize their legs and other components to allow the arm to follow suit effortlessly without being forced until the release point.

Pitching Tool #5: Overall Athleticism

Athleticism here refers to athletic coordination. Pitching requires a high degree of coordination, which can be difficult to teach. However, there are drills that can help coordination. Mechanics are different and perhaps are easier to improve upon. The mechanics are the various aspects that make up a pitch—the stance, the windup, and the throw—and athleticism is the ability to execute the mechanics.

A smooth throwing motion is just the starting point. It is the player's athleticism that allows him to control his body, like shifting weight, releasing the pitch, and creating explosive power at just the right time. This finely tuned kind of coordination allows the pitcher to deliver the specific pitch necessary to produce the desired results in an actual game.

As we mentioned previously, genetics can play a role in athleticism; however, training can overcome some genetic disadvantages. For example, the elasticity of muscles can vary from person to person. Some people are wired tighter than others, which will require more attention to loosen up and to guard against injury. The probability of injury tends to increase with less flexible players. Certain stretching routines can help increase flexibility. Consult a fascia stretch therapist for increased flexibility assistance. Players with more muscle elasticity and flexibility tend to be more coordinated.

Pitching Tool #6: Deception

Deception refers to how well the pitcher hides the ball and how early a hitter can recognize what pitch is being thrown, its movement, and its speed. Each of these can be disguised to some degree, which raises the deception quotient. The ability to deceive the hitter is an added value for any pitcher and can potentially help to make up for other deficiencies. If a pitcher's fastball maxes out at 85 mph but his deception rating is high, then the pitcher at 85 mph may be more successful than the pitcher at 90 mph without deception.

Hustle and Makeup

For all the positions and not just pitchers, there is an aspect of the game that can be a tipping point. It can be the difference between being in the lineup or not, between making the team or not. The significant role hustle can play in decision-making on the part of coaches and scouts cannot be overstated.

Any player can show hustle no matter how talented he is. Hustle is an attitude and a mindset. Baserunning is part of the mentality of hustle, which is an important aspect of the game that needs to be cultivated every day. Scouts are concerned about "false hustle," which is the phrase they use for the player who only tries hard when important people are watching. False hustle will always reveal itself eventually.

When true hustling is practiced every day, it becomes second nature and is not something that can be faked. This helps to create a competitive edge and may become a tipping point to get a player to the next level.

Hustle shows your passion to compete and to be in the game at all times. Coaches and scouts notice hustle. It makes a team better. It makes a player better. It demonstrates leadership and selflessness. It is easy to hustle when you get a hit, but what if you don't? What if you hit a fly ball or a groundball to someone? Do you still bust it down the line toward first base? Or do you half-heartedly trot to first?

If hustling is not part of your game, you need to make it so. Cultivating an attitude of hustle will make you a better player, and more importantly it will mold you into a better person.

Hustling, no matter what the outcome, reflects the player's true character on the field. As a player it may be difficult to appreciate how hustling could have such a significant impact, but not only does it have immediate effect, but it also has long-term implications.

Social media plays an integral part in judging a player's makeup as well. In the Internet age we live in, a player can ruin his career with social media posts, and many already have. It may not even be a post he wrote himself, but if he likes or follows a post from someone else that may be considered judgmental, racist, inhumane, or self-deprecating, it could incur long-term negative effects. A player must always be wary of the content he exposes himself to and what will be deemed as acceptable for him to post about thereafter. Every time he posts, it will be something the world may see, so he should take caution with each post.

Social media is an easy way to find out a player's character. Many can fake a job interview, but social media captures a lifestyle. Be very cautious about what you type, what pictures you post, who you're friends with, and who can see your posts. I'm not condoning hiding bad behavior by blocking people, but let's say a player and his friends have some inside joke they play and its true meaning is not malicious, but an outsider able to view it who doesn't know it's a joke may deem it malicious. How it's perceived is how it will often be taken, so always err on the side of caution.

There are other key components of what baseball insiders call "makeup." Though they may not mention it often, scouts and coaches are always watching for intangibles such as:

- How does a player carry himself when the team wins and when it loses?
- Is the player disrespectful to the umpire and/or his teammates when he's performing and/or not performing?
- Does the player have heart?
- How does he train and how often?
- Is he self-motivated or does he always need a coach barking at him?
- Does his mother carry his bat bag for him?
- Does his mother hand him numerous drinks, near the dugout, during the game?
- Lastly, is the player dedicated and willing to sacrifice above and beyond for baseball?

Makeup is a tool not often discussed, yet is huge for scouts. If a player excels at the traditional five tools but does not have the makeup scouts are looking for, he may be overlooked.

A friend of mine was hosting a tryout for a nationally known team. At the end of tryouts, he had one roster spot and two pitchers remaining. Both were lefties that threw in the mid 90s. In theory you could have flipped a coin and been happy with either choice. The coach's decision came down to the makeup factor.

Both pitchers seemed to have a solid makeup quotient about them, but my friend really wanted to assess how they would do in a time of crisis. Since that was not a part of his tryout, he improvised. He brought them both off the field and told them together that neither one of them had made the team. One player turned around, strutted off, and clearly communicated his frustration. The other player looked at the ground somberly, looked back up with glassy eyes, and respectfully said, "Thank you coach for the opportunity," and proceeded to shake the coach's hand firmly. The coach shook his hand and said, "Welcome aboard son. I had to cut one of you and I was basing it off your reaction whether it was respectful or not. You are the right character player for this particular team." In this case the importance of makeup won this young player a spot on the roster. This may be an unusual example, but it does illustrate how pivotal this factor can be.

Carry your own bat bag, exercise good sportsmanship even in defeat, take extra hits or pitches after practice, and pick up your own baseballs in the cages after you hit them and assist in helping someone else pick up theirs. Cultivating and adopting this kind of attitude will have profound implications beyond your playing days and will serve you well personally and professionally, both on and off the field.

Know How You Project

Now that you have an understanding of the profile, tools, and what scouts are looking for, you need to evaluate further the question of where you play. Know how you project.

What position on the field will give you the best opportunity to succeed in the long term? It is important that you are projecting at your primary position, the position you most often play.

You may have the quickest reflexes on the team and be incredibly efficient at third base. However, if you are 5'8" and do not hit for a ton of power, then you may want to seriously consider moving over to shortstop or second base.

Scouts will acknowledge your ability to make plays at third, but most of the time they will not imagine your talents elsewhere. A scout may not assume that if a player can play third base then he can play second base as well. Second requires more range and footwork than third base does. If a scout only watches you playing one position over and over again, then he may assume that you have minimal range or are compensating for other flaws. Either way, it does not leave a good impression and limits your options.

If you play shortstop, a scout will assume you can play second base, too, since both require excellent footwork and range. Of the two positions, the shortstop needs a stronger arm.

Can you project as a multiple-position player and have the same chance of succeeding?

Absolutely! And furthermore, your value as a player will increase. If you have the chance to move your position based on how you project, then do it. This should give you the best opportunity to succeed this year and in the future.

CHAPTER 8
AN EDGE

If opportunity doesn't knock, build a door.
—Milton Berle

Players and parents alike should know that there is no one thing that will determine whether or not you can make it to the next level. However, as today's game has become more sophisticated and complex, there are some options that perhaps can give players an edge. This chapter provides some insight that will equip you to make the best decisions for your situation.

Advantages

There are certain key factors that can give players an advantage. Some of these components are controllable and others are not. It is helpful to know what these advantages are as you grow in your understanding of how the baseball world works. Factors such as where you live, physical size, how often a player is seen by scouts and recruiters, as well as interpersonal skills, can give you an added edge.

Geography does give some players an advantage. The biggest states for baseball are Florida, California, Texas, and Georgia. The weather allows for mostly year-round play, which means scouts, coaches, and players have more opportunities to connect. These climates allow for players to practice and hone their skills consistently throughout the year. Over the years these states have produced large numbers of great athletes, which make them favored ground for recruiting. If you do not live in one of these four states, you may want to give priority to these areas when considering your college baseball options. The South is still considered the heart of baseball.

As mentioned previously, some scouts weigh a player's stats heavily, but most want to see the player in action. They are always eager to verify that the play matches the numbers. Actually seeing a player allows the scout to make a judgment regarding a player's potential. Some scouts come from the school of thought that if a young player shows enough potential, then the rest can be taught. This again underscores the importance of being seen by scouts.

The game is moving bigger and younger. Highly competitive high schools and club teams are actively being scouted for draft candidates. If the player has size, is young, and is putting up good numbers, then he may attract the attention of a scout.

One factor that can influence a scout is a player's height. Assuming talent and/or potential is present, then physical size often becomes one of the deciding factors. It is not like a tall player with no talent will win out over a more talented shorter player, but the physical makeup of a player is taken into account.

While talent is necessary, it is not always the determining factor. Consider this example: You are a scout and your job is evaluated based upon the recommendations and choices you make. You are looking at two shortstops. One is 5'9" and weighs 180 and the other is 6'4" and weighs 210. The 5'9" player is a stud but a little raw and choppy with his footwork. The 6'4" guy is strong, has a high exit velocity in batting practice, and is smooth on the field and looks the part, but his stats are not as impressive as the 5'9" player.

Who do you go with?

The unconventional choice would be to pick the 5'9" player. The 6'4" player has a higher upside and is an easier sell. Even if the 6'4" player does not work out, the leadership in the organization will not question why the scout selected him because he had potential and looked the part. This also means if this player does well, then everyone understands why. Either way, the scout has not put himself in a position where his judgment might be questioned. On the other hand, if the 5'9" player does not work out, then questions arise. This makes it more difficult for the scouting director to back the decision. Team leadership begins to ask, "Why did you pick him? Why this guy, when he is small, choppy, and average at best?" The 5'9" player is more of a risk for the scout and for his job.

Does this mean that anyone under 6'4" does not have a chance? Of course not, but it should highlight the importance of all the intangibles. If you do not meet the physical profile for your position, then you want to excel in every other category, so you make it almost impossible for a scout to overlook you, and you make it easy for the scout to sell you up his chain of command without jeopardizing his own reputation and job.

Recruiters—Good or Bad?

A recruiter is someone who charges money to make calls on your behalf to colleges and utilizes his connections for a player's benefit. In theory, this is a way to put you in the best possible position to receive the highest amount of visibility and scholarship money. Sadly, many recruiters do not have your best interest in mind. You need to weigh carefully the decision to use a recruiter.

If you decide to move forward, only go with someone who has an outstanding and proven track record.

What defines a proven track record?

- Years in business (it is probably best to stay away from any companies that are just starting out)
- Network of coaches known on a first-name basis. Anyone can cold call, but it does not mean you will ever get a return call or that the coach will even trust the recruiter's judgment.
- Past players and those players' success rate with the recruiter, to secure a college opportunity and excel. Be sure to contact those players' families to verify; don't just take the recruiter's word for it.
- College opportunities acquired for past players. Were they all Division III commits, or were there players who used this recruiter who ended up at higher-level programs?

One of the issues with recruiters is the difficulty in assessing their value. How much is he actually responsible for that player getting noticed? This is often difficult to know. The recruiter may have called the Division I college about a player, but the player lives in the South and plays in a highly competitive and known league where scouts and coaches hang out already. The reality is such a player is likely already on the college's radar and the recruiter did not have any influence, even though the recruiter may be taking the credit for it. This scenario shows the need to do your homework and research before signing on with a recruiter.

Also, if a recruiting service takes on players of all calibers, how can they possibly be of service? Put yourself in that recruiter's shoes. Let's say there's an average high school player who wants to pay for your services to play at the college level. What can you as the recruiter possibly say on that player's behalf? "So I have this kid who is average, really sub-par. You should take him." That's not going to work.

The recruiter can lie and say, "So, I got this stud who can really swing the bat, man! Top in the state! You're going to want him."

Yes, the college coach will be interested until he sees his lack of performance. Then the recruiter just lost a college source altogether because the college coach knows he's full of it and that player who was just pumped up with false hope just got cut too, assuming he even got that far.

So ask yourself, "What can an average recruiter do on my behalf that I can't do myself if he doesn't have a proven track record?"

Reputable recruiters or companies of recruiters will approach many players, but not everyone will be able to afford to pay for their services. It is always good to ask how many players they represent and at what positions they have the best rate of success. You want to ensure there are no inherent conflicts of interest with dozens of other players the recruiter is representing at your position. It's also prudent to see the colleges these players signed with and if they actually played. A recruiter can brag about his success rate of getting players to the next level, but maybe they are all DIII schools located in a place the player never wanted to go to anyway, or maybe the situations did in fact all pan out. Ask a lot of questions!

If a highly reputable recruiter approaches you and he has a proven track record with a network that can be beneficial to you, then you may want to consider this option. Please remember to choose your recruiting service wisely.

Showcases, Camps, and Showcase Teams

Showcases are baseball events where you can put your talent and skills on display for college coaches and/or professional scouts.

They are usually held at a sports training facility, field, or college or pro complex. Some of them are worthwhile, but many of them are just money makers for those hosting the event. Be selective and strategic. Do not go into these events blindly.

As a parent or player you may view showcases as an opportunity to get noticed or recruited. However, coaches and pro scouts sometimes use these occasions to weed out and eliminate players as opposed to recruiting them. If you are a standout player, perform well under pressure, and profile well at your position, then showcases may be a good option for you.

If you do not perform well at practices or in tryout settings, then showcases probably are not for you. Think about it. Maybe you hit a double at the showcase and you run the bases. This is great! The only problem is, so did 35 other players.

What if a college or pro coach asks you to attend a particular showcase? This is different, especially if you produce there. Now those hits you get are more meaningful because you know they were watching you.

> ### Tip!
> If you receive a personal invitation to
> participate at a college camp when you are
> in high school, and you have legally spoken to the
> college coach or know he is already
> interested, then usually it is to your advantage
> to attend. The coaches are looking for
> opportunities to get to know you better.

A word of caution here: Please do not throw common sense out the window when it comes to making baseball decisions. If you have been personally invited to camp by a coach and it is extremely expensive, unless you have grown to know the coach well, then you need to do your homework on the camp. Pick up the phone and call whoever is running the camp to find out more information. Make sure the camp is worth the expense before committing to attend. Ask questions, such as, "Why is the camp more costly than others and what is the value added to those who attend?" Inquire about what percentage of participants become scholarship players at the college level thereafter. This is just a small sampling of questions that can be asked.

It would have been more beneficial for me if I had been more selective in what camps and showcases I attended. For example, one camp had its own system of metrics to rate players. However, this system was quite limiting. Because it was too narrow, scouts used this camp to confirm their own rankings of players who were already being watched and did not view it as a viable means to identify new talent. Before attending, you should ask about the metrics and matrices used to rate players.

Besides camps and showcases, there are two showcase teams that are highly recognized in the scouting world: Area Code Baseball and East Coast Pro. Area Code has its hub in Long Beach, California, while East Coast Pro is located in Tampa, Florida. Area Code is a nationwide entity with two of their eight teams located in California, while East Coast Pro has teams in the central United States and throughout the East Coast. Area Code and East Coast Pro have many of the best high school players in the country on their rosters.

To be invited to an Area Code tryout, a player must be recommended by someone who is a major-league scout and a part of the Major League Baseball Scouting Bureau. Even then, there's no guarantee the player will even be invited to the tryout regardless of what scout recommended him. Also, if he does get invited and has an excellent tryout, there's still no guarantee he will make the team because of the amount of competition. The tryouts are usually free since they are "invite-only" and many scouts, agents, and advisors are in attendance.

The Area Code teams are comprised of roughly 25 players and each team scopes out talent over a large area. One team known as the "Northeast" has some of the best players from as far north as Maine and as far south as West Virginia, and every state in between. The teams are generally coached by area scouts from that particular area of the country.

It's not easy to make the team, and some positions may already be locked up prior to the tryout. One player was an All-American who hit seven home runs in batting practice and still wasn't asked back. Another player, as a catcher, threw a 1.81 pop time down to second and hit two home runs and also didn't make it. However, his advisor called on his behalf and Area Code issued him an additional tryout. Sometimes clout can go a long way.

East Coast Pro has a similar business model to Area Code. The scouts invite the players to the tryout and the process begins. Sometimes a scout will host a personal tryout and then from there the player may get asked to the East Coast Pro tryout where scouts from all MLB teams are in attendance. Like Area Code, East Coast Pro keeps roughly 25 players per team. It's an honor to be invited to either Area Code or East Coast Pro, and if given the opportunity, a player should definitely attend the tryout. A decent number of current and former pros have played for these teams.

> ## Tip!
> When it comes to showcases, "invitation only"
> ones are often more prestigious. It is
> also good to ask about the number of Division
> I, II, and III college coaches who will be in
> attendance, pro scouts in attendance, as
> well as other players who will be there.

The Just Experience

One showcase I attended was by invitation only and quite expensive. At the time in 2005, it was known as the Best of Virginia showcase. It was extremely beneficial. I met a number of Division I college coaches, made good connections, and I learned a great deal. One lesson I learned is that it is not always about talent; it is also about available slots on a team at any given time.

From this particular showcase, I received an invitation to attend a Coastal Carolina camp that fall (2016 College World Series champions), which I did. Afterwards, Coach Gilmore was eager to sign me, but his main issue was that I was a senior in high school and he had been recruiting and watching other players at his camps since they were freshmen. He already had a second baseman (major leaguer David DeJesus's brother Michael) coming in on scholarship, but had he known of my availability sooner, I would have been a more viable option and could have competed for those scholarship spots. Success from this particular showcase led me to call Liberty University and leverage Coastal's interest against Liberty's which eventually led me to commit to Liberty, where I ended up playing in the same Big South Conference as Coastal Carolina.

Another lesson I learned was that attending the camps of your top college choices early on in high school (freshman and sophomore years) will increase your visibility, allow you to establish rapport with some of the college coaches, and ultimately should create more scholarship opportunities for you when the time comes.

Tip!
College coaches will want to see you play and get to know you personally so they can accurately assess your attitude, makeup, and character.

To put things in perspective, in most cases it is better to spend money on going to the college camps (even better if you're personally invited to them) year after year, rather than attending any random showcase that is available. Be strategic and smart about how you invest in these opportunities.

Coaches may call you from time to time after the legal deadline if you are being heavily recruited. Please be sure that you, as the player, are talking to the coach and not your parents. These teams are not recruiting your mother or father. They want to hear from the person they are actively pursuing. Are you personable, likeable, and can you hold a complete thought? Again, these are all important pieces of a puzzle when coaches are thinking about how you will add value to their team.

Remember, players are an investment for both the coaches and their colleges. Coaches are always juggling multiple priorities. Are you the kind of student-athlete that will represent their institution well? How much scholarship money should be offered based upon the player's talent, the team's needs, and the player's ability to mesh well with the team?

Just like baseball skills, these intangibles are things that can be developed but need to be practiced. It may be hard to connect these things to baseball, but it is important to understand how coaches' logic works. If you cannot carry on a conversation, then maybe there is a chance you will not remember the signs or plays. Yes, people skills and memory are different. However, there is overlap, and when a coach is on the prowl for red flags, he may not take the time to parse every thought. Coaches realize that their players represent them, and they want to be well represented.

Your talent is the reason he is talking to you in the first place, but there is a great deal of talent out there, so honing your interpersonal skills, keeping your grades high, and being a team player will increase your opportunities for serious consideration by coaches.

What Else Can I Do?

Unless you live in one of the top states for recruiting (Florida, California, Texas, and Georgia), or are on a club team that plays tournaments in these regions, it's unlikely that a representative of the college or pro team of your dreams has seen you play.

Phone calls will only get you so far. If you want a call back, they need to know who you are. Again, this is why attending college camps and establishing relationships are so important. You could also be a part of a tournament for exposure like Perfect Game, Ripken, Diamond Nation, Sports at the Beach (Rehobeth Beach, Delaware), Baseball Heaven, or Cooperstown (Dreams Park and All-Star Village). Make sure you comply with NCAA rules (see the NCAA website) about when you are allowed to contact and be contacted by a college coach.

After your initial contact with the recruiting coach, keep in touch utilizing a variety of methods. Ask a parent politely to videotape a couple of your at-bats in a game. When you string together several good at-bats, send the video to the coach and leave a message or email him to let him know the video is on its way.

Also, find out if the coaches will be visiting your state anytime soon on a recruiting trip. Try to arrange a day when they can come see you play in a game during your high school or summer league season.

Don't worry if you go 0-for-4. If you hustled, showed a positive attitude, and did some little things right, this will go a long way to making a good impression. The coaches know that not every game is perfect. Besides, they have your stats and accolades because you have been emailing them clippings of your successes over the past several years.

You can create a baseball résumé (see Appendix A) and send them headlines for every game-winning hit. This will help keep you in the forefront of the coaches' minds.

As you make opportunities to connect with coaches, there are specific questions you should be asking them:

- Am I one of your priority guys (see Chapter 9)?
- How many freshmen started for you last year and do you potentially see me getting significant playing time for

you as a freshman? (It's rare that a freshman plays, but it's still good to find out.)
- What position(s) do you see me playing for you?
- Would you anticipate scholarship money being available for me?

All of these questions are perfectly appropriate and will yield a tremendous amount of information about how that team views you. Don't forget that playing ball at the next level involves two parties making decisions. The first is the team who is interested, but the second party is you and your family. You may be fortunate to have multiple opportunities, which make it all the more important for you to understand what a specific team has in mind for you and how you can fit into its program.

These kinds of discussions with coaches will also give you insight into what it will be like to interact with them. Coaches and programs do not change when you join the team, so what you see is what you will encounter as a player.

You should also be asking yourself specific questions to help narrow down your focus. This personal assessment will help you make the best all-around decision for your future:

- Major (Does the school interested in you even offer the major of your choice and does the school you're interested in have your major?)
- Network (For your intended major, what type of internship and post-college job opportunities does the college/university provide?
- Proximity (Do you want to be a day's drive away from your family or do you not mind taking a flight home and the cost incurred?)

- Depth of the program per positions. (How many players do they normally carry and how do you fit into their equation of potential playing time? How well did the players produce who are currently in front of you per position and what year are they?)
- Liberal/conservative views that you will become indoctrinated with. "You are what you eat." The more you hear and listen to administration teach/preach their worldviews, the more you will retain and apply them yourself.
- Personal connection with head coach as well as assistant coaches. Find out their philosophies, and who you will be working with on a daily basis, and make sure it's a solid fit.

After narrowing your choices down, if you still can't decide on the best fit for you between two schools, take out a pencil and paper. Draw a line directly down the middle of the sheet to divide the paper into two columns. In the first column, write all the "pros" and in the second column write all the "cons." In addition to the issues covered above, also think about the following factors:

- Number of students enrolled on campus
- Size of campus
- Ratio of students to teachers in the classroom
- Male to female ratio
- Whether or not you can drive your car on campus as a freshman or not
- Aesthetics and condition of the dorms, classroom buildings, and athletic facilities

Some of the less important issues may be very important for you. Prioritize your list specifically for you. Be creative, and think inside and outside the box. After you're done writing, take a look at each sheet. Chances are, one will have slightly or significantly more "pros" and fewer "cons" than the other and you will be able to identify your best choice.

If you're undecided on what you really want to do with your life, there are two philosophies. One is to do what you love and the other is to do it for the money. Here's the problem with both of those. If you pursue a career solely in what you "love," if you cannot provide for yourself or your family, your "love" will become short-lived. In addition, what you do day in and day out, no matter what you do, takes its toll somehow/someway. If you pursue a career for the money, chances are you will be miserable and you are sacrificing your well-being and others for financial stability. What if there was another solution? Well, there is. Research the top 25 best hiring/paying jobs and find the one that may resonate with you the best. Start there and attempt to mesh the love with the financial stability and build on that.

CHAPTER 9
TRICKY SCENARIOS

If you come to a fork in the road, take it.
—Yogi Berra

The player who is capable of playing at the college level, if not the pros, will encounter any number of situations that need to be navigated wisely. What are the advantages of being a "priority guy" or someone who has "favored status"? What if you don't have favored status? What if the head coach who recruited you leaves before you arrive? Can being drafted out of high school ever be a bad thing? Does it matter what college division you play in?

The Advantages of Being a "Priority Guy"

If a coach finds a way to get money for you, congratulations, you are one of his priority guys!

To an extent, you almost force his hand to play you at some point, because he would have a lot of explaining to do to the athletic director if you are a backup on a 75 percent scholarship.

When you arrive at the park and you know you are starting every day, there is much less pressure on you to produce. Your success rate is likely to be higher. More often than not, the coach will stick with you through good times and bad.

I've been the everyday guy . . . and I haven't been. Times were much easier when I was the priority guy, knowing my performance would not determine whether I lost that status. Priority guys tend to have less pressure on the field and less pressure in the classroom. If you don't have to worry about winning a spot, your stress levels go down.

It can be easy to abuse your status as a priority guy by not working hard and slacking off. Doing so will only hurt yourself and your team. Some coaches will sense it and might go as far as releasing you from the team to free up the scholarship money for others and to prevent you from setting a bad example for other players. Depending on your contract with the school and the amount of money involved, coaches can and will find a way to release you if they want to, so don't give them any reason to ever consider it.

However, the coach isn't guaranteed to play you just because you have favored status as an investment in the program. He may get flack if he doesn't, but he still doesn't have to.

Let's say you are the head coach of a Division I college baseball team and the infield you have is stellar. The season goes well and you get to the championship game, and your infield makes great defensive plays and hits in the clutch. Your infielders proved to you they work well together and they will produce in high- and low-pressure situations. When the next year rolls around, you have your infielders back because they were sophomores. A transfer infielder comes in, hits well, fields well, and expects to start. Where do you put him? You can't put him anywhere in the infield, because the "If it ain't broke, you don't fix it" theory is in place. If the new player can't be made into an outfielder, catcher, or DH, then he will not play. There's not enough room and you may not want to mess with the dynamics of the infield.

From day one, that transfer player had little chance of starting in the infield, and he should have done the research before he transferred and expected to play. The coach is committed to building a team that has choices in the event someone gets hurt, and the future of his program is a priority, so he won't shoot himself in the foot by admitting to a recruit that they won't be a starter. This is why research is important. Never fall into the trap of assuming the best players will start. The best guys don't always play.

If you are in a situation similar to the transfer student above, see how much playing time last year's infielders as a whole received when considering that program. The numbers will show some of the coach's style.

When a coach has an abundance of talent and he's trying to utilize it to push each player, then you are in a good situation. This "roving" scenario involves four starting players for third, short, and second and potentially four starting players in the outfield.

Not all players start at once of course, but you have one more priority guy in the outfield and one more priority guy in the infield than needed. This makes the players have to play up to their potential, or they could be the odd man out.

The coach usually won't push it to the point where one 0-for-4 game means that player is benched for a week. The coach will simply rotate the players depending upon who is hot and who is not and won't sit them for more than a game or two.

If a coach deems the roving scenario is the best route to go because of the team's depth, then he should communicate this game plan before the season starts, so his players know what to expect, but informing them that certain players can solidify their positions at any time. The roving scenario can be a successful strategy if a coach has the recruiting ability or program to acquire enough quality players, and if the players buy into the team style of play.

If communicated to the players properly beforehand, the roving scenario also keeps players happy because they will get plenty of playing time, while given a day off to rest every now and then depending on production. If the players are team-driven, they will understand this style.

Once again, it has to be emphasized prior to the start of the season that the players are all priorities, otherwise no one will get comfortable and all will be on edge. A good coach will make it known that if one player slacks off, or consistently doesn't produce, then he might not play. It reassures the players to work hard, but also lets them know they can relax and if they trust in their abilities, it will work out just fine for those that earn it.

The roving scenario also depends on the versatility of the players on the team. Sometimes coaches mix and match, and some players rove while others are fixtures at particular positions.

Under these strict circumstances, assuming you have done the research about the program, it might be all right to assume some playing time could be available for you if you produce.

What If the Head Coach Leaves?

During your research, it is wise to consider how many players were drafted out of that high school or college.

What were their statistics and did they get a shot at playing in the pros? That's an important question when considering your future in baseball.

Two guys come to mind when I think of this scenario. They were basically the same age and played the same position. They went to two separate Division I programs south of the

Mason-Dixon Line and they both played about the same caliber of competition. One hit in the high .200s in college and one in the high .300s. The one who hit in the high .200s was drafted in the 21st round and the one who hit in the high .300s was undrafted. The one who hit in the high .300s ended up getting signed as a free agent after the draft, while the one who hit in the high .200s ended up making it all the way to Triple A! He never had a good year with the bat in his pro career, but because of the college he attended and the credibility of the coach at that college, he was given all the chances in the world to make it, and to his credit still had enough tools to climb the ladder, which is why he was drafted in the first place.

Both players ended up on the same team in Independent ball, and guess who started and did better overall? The player that hit in the high .300s for a Division I college, but never played affiliated baseball. Scenarios like this happen more often than not. It's important to attend a college that has credibility in the scouting world and a coach who is well known and respected in the industry.

Tip!

I advise against attending a college if you are not the head coach's recruit or he isn't aware of who you are. Also, if a new coach is coming in your first year, then you need to do extensive research on him. If you are absolutely adamant about attending a particular program despite the coaching change, research is essential to find out as much detail as you can about your soon-to-be new head coach.

When athletic directors hire new coaches, they ask questions before making their final decision. You need to ask these questions too. Why did he leave the previous place? What are his credentials?

The last thing you want to do is trust that things will work out, when you are unaware of major details that will directly impact your future.

When I was recruited by the previous head coach of Liberty University, I thought since a new head coach was coming in that I would have an equal opportunity for playing time since he wouldn't have any favorites. For the most part, I was right. In fact, I worked hard and produced enough in the off-season to become the opening day starter against University of Virginia as a freshman. But I was missing some other valuable pieces of information. As a head coach who was trying to build a program, he would bring many of his high school and junior college recruits from his former location to the new one. Some students from the former college would even follow him too. I also failed to ask some key questions:

Why did he leave his previous college? Was it a forced resignation?

Did the boys who played for him in the past like him?

Did many players get drafted (thus proving he has good relations with scouts)?

Did many players receive athletic rewards such as All Conference, All-American or other valuable player status (proving he battles for his players when those meetings come)? Not having the answers to those questions came back to bite me in the end.

When I was looking at colleges, it was too late to do all the research I should have done, but I did look into how many players were drafted per year. Every year it seemed there were a few guys drafted, and the year before I went to Liberty, five guys were drafted.

The summer before college, I got word the coach was no longer returning. If this happens to you, you may want to reconsider committing to that school unless you have met the new coach or know something about him from your research.

If you're already at the school when the new coach comes in, you might want to consider transferring unless the new coach knew of you, or has recruited and conversed with you in some way and is willing to give you equal opportunity.

Even then, staying with the new coach is risky, and here is why:

First, we already know the new coach will bring in his own players to try to build his own program. He's going to try to call on his past or current recruits and let them know where he will now be the head coach.

Secondly, everything you learned from the previous college coach may get thrown out the window, from small things such as signs, to large things such as philosophies and connections. This might not fit into your style of play; you were recruited by a different coach who chose you because you fit well with *his* program.

Thirdly, it might take the new coach a year to four years to build a decent program. Do you want to be a part of his rebuilding years? He will want to win, but he will have some leeway if he loses the first year or two because in his mind, as well as in the minds of the athletic director and administration, he is playing with mostly players that aren't his recruits anyway. New coaches typically have leverage to stick around and prove what they can do over a multi-year period. These are all factors that affect your aspirations as a future pro ballplayer. However, if the new head coach was hired from within the current administration (previously an assistant) so you still have a relationship with him, then he may be worth staying for.

One scenario involved a 33rd-round draft pick out of high school with an 80 percent college scholarship offer. We will call him John. John had a choice. John was recruited by one of the assistant coaches at a big Division I school, and was also drafted out of high school and offered some money to play for the Pirates organization. John took a huge gamble by committing to the Division I school, because a new coach would be coming in, and he had other college scholarships and the Pirates organization as options. In the fall of his freshman year, he was hitting over .400. He had a powerful upright stance that gave him the leverage to hit the ball 400 feet. John had an excellent glove and perfect body type for a professional first baseman.

He was a lanky lefty/lefty, 6'4", 205 pounds, who had excellent footwork at first base with immense power at the plate. That winter, the college coaches messed with him offensively. They changed his stance to make it wider and shorter. They changed his philosophy, emphasizing his top hand so he would hit more groundballs instead of deep drives to the gaps. He was forced to run laps if he hit a fly ball in batting practice, and he even ran a lap for hitting a home run in batting practice, which is absurd. John was a prototypical middle-of-the-lineup power guy, and the head coach was taking him completely out of his style of play.

John was also the type of player who played well with positive reinforcement, which implied that he could potentially crumble under negative reinforcement. The new coach was more of a negative reinforcement type, as he was under the impression that he could motivate through a "no one ever being good enough" style. In a nutshell, the coaching staff was a bad fit for John and he posted numbers in the low .200s that spring. At every level there are excellent coaches and poor coaches, even the college level. Some coaches are on a power trip to try to prove something and some just go with the flow, while others care immensely about the development and success of each player.

Keep in mind that John was not the head coach's recruit. So after that season, there was another first baseman recruited from California and that new recruit started over John. Scouts approached John after batting practice and told him they were looking forward to seeing him play in the game. He told them, "I'm sorry, but I'm not a starter."

As a reserve, during his sophomore year, John hit over .300. The next year John was gone from the team altogether while the head coach stuck with his own recruit at first base. John never played his last two years of Division I college ball, and the scouts moved on.

After two years of not even picking up a baseball, John suddenly had the urge to play again and drove himself to a pro try-out. He signed a professional spring training contract. He called me immediately to inform me of the awesome news and I told him how proud of him I was. He didn't make it out of spring training, but scouts saw his tools and were willing to give him a chance. Imagine that!

The new college coach didn't mesh well with John. But was it the coach's fault, or was it John's fault for going into a program without information on the new head coach? By not doing extensive research before making the decision that would eventually make or break his baseball career, John took a gamble and lost.

As you already know, I went to the school with the new coach because I thought I would get a fair shot at the infield, since he would be evaluating everyone from scratch with "new eyes." Not a bad way of thinking, but still flawed to an extent because I didn't factor in scholarship money (priority guys) and the new guys that would be brought in.

Even if my way of thinking proved true, I had overlooked a very important issue . . . connections!

Did the coach have any at all?

Did scouts even respect his opinion?

Did he push for the players to get opportunities?

The new coach did away with Scout Day altogether. His rationale, which he shared freely with us, was that none of us were good enough to play at the next level anyway. Whether he meant it or not, he still said it.

On Scout Day pro scouts representing every organization come to watch you perform for the day. My freshman year every team was present; my sophomore year only the New York Mets scout was there, and when I ran a 6.59 60-yard dash, my head coach told the scout that it wasn't a real time that translated to the field. Then, by junior year, we didn't have a Scout Day at all.

It is unfortunate that players I played with during those five years—some of whom broke the records of players who had been good enough to be drafted in previous years (some in the top 10 rounds)—still could not get an opportunity at the next level. I had the single-season hit record with 94 hits in 60 games and the fielding assist record at 175 assists in 60 games, and in 2004 I was 12th in the nation in hardest to strike out according to the NCAA (Dustin Pedroia was 23rd that year).

That is the price you might end up paying if you do not do your research!

This was no one's fault but mine. I should have done my homework and researched the history of the coach before making the commitment. Hindsight is always 20/20, and experience is the best teacher. Learn from my mistake as well as John's.

The Just Experience

Liberty University ended up hiring an excellent new head coach in 2007, and by 2013 they were ranked 26th in the nation by the NCAA and had many players drafted over that span.

What is the solution you might ask?

If you are already in John's situation, you may be in too deep. If you decide not to transfer, then you will have to bite the bullet and hope for the best.

My client, Mike, found himself in the same predicament at a Division III school. My advice to him regarding his "cookie-cutter" coach was the following: When the coach says your bat has to start here in your stance before you load, he's full of it. Just watch any big-league game. The hitters all have different stances for a reason, "comfort ability." Anyone who plays at a higher level understands this and respects this. So when coaches try and make every hitter the same, they may be making a big mistake.

A coach should never, *never* make an adjustment on a player without proving why that adjustment will give the player better results than what he is already getting. If the coach cannot prove why, he's teaching based on philosophy rather than fact. Your way could be just as beneficial if not even better.

How do you explain this to the coach? The reality is you can't. If you question him, you are labeled as uncoachable. If you are correct, you are attacking that coach's pride and ego, so it's a lose/lose for you anyway.

You have to nod your head, say yes coach, and still do your own thing.

If he asks, "Why aren't you doing what I say?," your response is "I am working on it, but it's going to take time to get this down. It's a different feel."

You should always try it. Maybe you'll love it, maybe you'll hate it. Trying it once or twice in practice doesn't mean you have to use the new stance every time. Plus, it will also get him off your back for the time being. That way, when you go back to the stance you're comfortable with and you rope your next double, you can shake the coach's hand and thank him for the adjustments. Maybe it did actually work for you and it's a genuine thank you, or maybe it didn't. Either way, it may get the coach off your back to shift his focus to other players. If he doesn't know what he's talking about anyway, he will try and take credit, not realizing you didn't do what he said, and then everybody wins.

If you start off slow with production at the plate, more often than not coaches will attack you like vultures and try to change your hitting style. If you continue to not get hits, they will stay on your case until you produce. Do your research by not committing to a program if a coach's philosophy doesn't mesh well with yours. Ask the current players on the team before you commit. If you don't do this research, you could have a four-year battle ahead of you.

Is Being Drafted Out of High School a Good Thing or a Bad Thing?

What a moment! You work hard your whole life and the moment has come. As incredible and awesome as this moment is, you have to step back and think rationally. You have to figure out if it's the right decision or not to accept the draft and pass up the opportunity to go to college.

Referring back to the John situation, it's easy to say in hindsight that he should have accepted the draft. However, with the right college coach who could continue to develop what John had started, college could have turned out to be the right move for him. What about some other players I played with or know? How did it work out for them?

Brent was a varsity shortstop as a freshman at my high school, Saint Joseph Regional. His uncle was a former shortstop for the Atlanta Braves organization. Brent was a talented player with phenomenal makeup. When Brent was a senior in high school, he was drafted late in the draft, 47th round. He also had a scholarship offer to George Mason University. Brent took the college route and was never drafted again, so he ended up losing his one shot at the pros. But as a late-round draftee in high school, it might have been risky to turn down the college that might provide him with future baseball opportunities and the chance to earn a degree. Remember, if Brent had signed a pro contract, he would no longer have been eligible to play college baseball and would have most likely lost any college scholarship that was on the table.

Some players have negotiated pro contracts that will cover part of their college tuition if they don't make it to the "Bigs," but that doesn't happen often unless you are a top prospect and have negotiating power.

Jan Baldee was a 17-year-old shortstop in the Houston Astros organization who relocated from the Netherlands. He didn't get one hit all of spring training 2008. But, he was given a $25,000 signing bonus out of high school and at least one scout viewed him as a solid "profile" for shortstop. He stood 6'2" and had a rubber arm, so the Astros figured, why not invest a little in a young guy to see how we can develop him? A small amount risk for some potential reward since he's young and there's not much money involved, so why not?

Put yourself in that player's shoes and you take that offer 100 percent of the time.

The pro organization is investing some money in you, proving they want to develop you out of high school. At the age of 17 and from the Netherlands where baseball isn't huge, with money invested in you, what do you have to lose?

Because he was a small investment, Jan lasted to a second professional year, but only batted .024 in 18 games for the Astros of the Gulf Coast League. He only had one hit in 41 at-bats and struck out 24 times. He also made seven errors in 29 chances in eight games as a shortstop. They released him when he was 19 years old, but felt it necessary to give him a little time to showcase what he could do because they invested in him.

Rob Kaminsky is a local guy from my alma mater, Saint Joseph Regional, who was drafted in the first round out of high school by the Cardinals, 28th pick overall. He signed for just shy of $1.8 million.

If you are drafted that high, you have a strong chance to make it to the top. Also, the fact that the organization gave him so much money makes Rob one of their priority money guys, also increasing the chance they will use him for trade bait for other prospects or current big leaguers. He will have every chance to succeed, because no organization will just throw away $1.8 million.

Rob is in the driver's seat and the pressure is not on him; it is on the organization or any future organization who acquires him. If Rob's performance is average, he should still have a path up the ladder. If Rob performs well, then he will move up the ladder even faster. Most of the time, those who receive smaller signing bonuses will receive fewer opportunities. The organizations have to protect their investments, so if you have the opportunity to become an investment, then use that to your advantage: Negotiate and sign.

But do you always sign? Let's say you were a left-side infielder in the late 1990s/early 2000s and you were just drafted high by the New York Yankees out of high school, and you also have college scholarship opportunities. Your parents are going crazy, and you can't wait to accept that $500,000 the Yankees just offered you to play for your favorite team. But hang on a second. What about your future? Let's view the Yankees in that time frame, shall we? Scott Brosius was at third base and he had just been the World Series MVP. Derek Jeter was at short, and even if you can play second, there's Chuck Knoblauch and then Robbie Cano ready to take over a few years later. Tino Martinez was at first base.

Where would you fit into this equation?

You could consider taking the college scholarship opportunity and hope another organization drafts you in college. The other alternatives are to sign with the Yankees and completely change your position to outfield (let's not forget about David Justice, Bernie Williams, Paul O'Neill, and later on Gary Sheffield among others at the time), or hope to get traded to another organization.

Either way it's a crapshoot, so maybe you sign even if it's mostly to get the $500,000 and invest it. But let's face it, after taxes, how long can you make that money last?

But there's a reason why many professional athletes are broke two to four years after they leave pro ball. Even if you break up your money into yearly installments, so you claim less yearly, you're still paying a large sum in taxes. Eventually, your principal amount of cash will deplete, too. So, maybe the college scholarship opportunity is the best way to go.

These decisions are tough to make, but it's wise to always view them from every angle possible and figure out the best plan of attack for your future.

College Divisions—How Much Do They Matter?

The college division you come from can play a vital role in how you compete at the pro level. The divisions include Division I, Division II, Division III, National Association of Intercollegiate Athletics (NAIA), and Junior College . . . which in turn has three divisions in and of itself.

Division I: Second basemen generally need to be between 5'10" and 6'2" and weigh between 185 and 205 pounds. Shortstops need to be a tad larger at a minimum of 6'0" and 175 pounds and no max on the height with maybe a weight cap of around 220 for a large shortstop. The muscle weight is more significant than the height for second basemen, simply because the more power behind your bat speed, the harder the exit velocity is off the bat and the less of a chance your opponent has to react to catch the ball.

Both positions should have solid range and footwork that is polished and not choppy. The 60-yard time for strong Division I schools should be 6.5–6.75 seconds (generally sub-3.9 home to first time). For "soft" or less competitive Division I colleges, 6.9 seconds or less is desirable, thus transferring to a 4.2 seconds or less home to first time. Throwing velocity should be 85 mph or higher as a shortstop and 83 mph or higher as a second baseman.

For corner infielders the breakdown is as follows: Height is usually 6'1" to 6'5", minimum of 200 pounds, with emphasis on power numbers. Fielding is important here, but overshadowed by sheer size and power to produce RBIs with a high slugging percentage. Average is important, but power is a larger factor and can overshadow lower averages. It is important for the first baseman to have above average footwork and be able to pick the ball well over at first.

Running speed is least important for corner positions.

At third, the arm needs to be equivalent to that of a shortstop or slightly less powerful . . . 85 mph and up should suffice. At first base, you can get away with 80 mph and up depending upon the program, since you won't have to make that many hard/long throws.

Outfielders, particularly center fielders, need to run extremely fast at the Division I level to gain maximum ground coverage. Corner outfielders usually run the 60-yard dash in 6.8 seconds or less and center fielders 6.7 or less, and all outfielders will be expected to have good range and get a good jump on the ball off the bat. Most Division I outfielders will be over 6'0" tall and weigh 185 to 215 pounds. Their home-to-first time is generally 4.1 seconds or less. Most Division I outfielders will have a plus arm, throwing 88 mph and up. They need to hit for average and some power. If they have plus power (16 or more doubles and 10 or more home runs in a season) then it's a bonus and they can provide less speed.

Division I catchers need to have about a 1.95-seconds-or-less pop time down to second base consistently and accurately, which usually transfers to a minimum of 85 mph. A catcher who throws a 2.0 may be okay if he shows good signs of projection (meaning he's still in the middle stages of puberty and hasn't fully developed, maybe his dad is a monster and there's size potential down the road, or maybe his body frame can hold another 30 pounds of muscle but hasn't been maximized yet). Catchers' heights vary, and I have played against some solid catchers under 6'0" tall, but most are over 6'0" and weigh 190 pounds and up. Catchers should maintain a solid presence behind the plate, get the ball quickly and firmly back to the pitcher, keep the game moving at a solid pace for the pitcher and defense, receive the ball well, and have few if any passed balls. Offensively a catcher should hit for average and power, but there's leeway here for a catcher who is a phenom defensively. That catcher will have more room for error offensively and vice versa.

Pitching standards vary for lefties and righties. For Division I lefties, velocity does not need to be as high. Because lefties are always in demand, lefties can throw as low as 84 and hit spots, yet righties usually can't throw lower than 86. Most righty starters at the Division I level will sit in the upper 80s and touch the low 90s consistently. The higher the velocity, the less the third pitch will matter, and secondary pitches do not have to be unhittable if the pitcher has a high-velocity fastball with movement. Both lefties' and righties' ERAs should be under 3.00, and they should average over 1 strikeout per inning pitched. Pitchers should also be able to locate two if not three out of their four pitches consistently and should have double the amount of strikeouts as walks.

Division II and Division III: Take the Division I information and tweak it down slightly for Division II (e.g., for Division I lefty pitchers at 85 mph, figure 83 mph, and for outfielders running 6.7 seconds, figure 6.8–6.9 seconds) and then tweak it down slightly again for Division III. Then you will have a rough idea of how standards differ among the top three divisions.

NAIA: NAIA colleges are four-year schools just like Division I, II, and III programs, and many NAIA programs are comparable to Division II and high Division III programs, so run the above numbers accordingly.

Junior College: Junior colleges are two-year schools, commonly referred to as "Ju-Cos." There are different levels of competition within the junior college world, just like Division I, II, and III in the NCAA.

If you attend a Ju-Co, you should either have hopes of getting drafted and not staying in school for three or four years, or hopes of getting a better college opportunity after your two years of Ju-Co. In junior college you are draft-eligible after the first and second year, and you also have the option of transferring in as a junior to an NCAA Division I, II, or III program, depending upon how many credits transfer. This allows you to be draft-eligible for four straight years. Ju-Co may be a solid choice for many players for many reasons. Let's say you are a player who gets drafted in the 12th round out of high school and they are offering you some money, but not enough money for you to make a decision to commit to that MLB team. If you think you are good enough to be a Top 10 rounder, then maybe it is in your best interest to go to a local competitive Ju-Co, or if you're feeling up for the challenge to network in Texas, Georgia, Florida, or California (where most of the top Ju-Cos are located), post the numbers, and get drafted the next year in the Top 10 rounds, which will mean more signing money, and more of an investment in you as a player in their organization. Also, remember that if you start in a Ju-Co out of high school, you now have up to four potential years after high school to get drafted as opposed to a Division I, II, or III program, which will only allow you to get drafted junior or senior year, or if you turn age 21 before a certain deadline.

Here's another scenario. What if you are a talented high school player, but for whatever reason you don't get many looks or exposure from any Division I programs, or your grades don't match the university that your heart is set on? If this is the case, then you can talk to some Ju-Cos and see if they have any interest in you. If you go the Ju-Co route and you do well, not only are you draft-eligible yearly, but you also now open up more doors for Division I possibilities. After your second year at the Ju-Co, assuming you performed as well as you anticipated both on the field and in the classroom, chances are you can now transfer to a Division I program, rather than accepting the Division II offer that was on the table back in high school.

There are competitive Division II programs and soft Division II programs, just as there are for Division I and Division III. But remember how scouts view the competition. A guy who is blowing guys away in Division II would most likely not be as highly rated as a guy with good numbers at a Division I school.

Here is a high school example that shows why you should shoot to go as high as you can possibly go:

During my sophomore year of high school, I played American Legion ball for my high school summer team and we were competitive, advancing far in the state. The team was comprised of the best players from surrounding towns in northern New Jersey. We dominated the area that summer and I hit .590 for that program.

My senior year, Pascack Hills broke off from the Legion team and did its own thing. Pascack Hills was the public school for the town that I grew up in, and the competition and summer league they were in wasn't as solid as my parochial school baseball program. I wanted to play my senior year with my town friends who were playing on the Pascack Hills team, so I opted to play there instead of St. Joseph's that summer before I left for Liberty University.

I expected to hit .700 that summer, since I hit .590 the summer before in a tougher league. However, I hit .548. I hit the ball just as hard and consistently that summer as the summer prior. That's when I realized that you can only hit the ball so hard and so consistently. There are still nine fielders making plays just as there are at the other levels. So, if you are a solid player who can handle a high level of competition, then it is wise to go to that higher level, because the difference in numbers may not break down to be as extreme as you thought they would have been. Not to mention, in a more competitive program, you have other solid players in the lineup to back you up. If you're a stud in a less competitive program, pitchers can force you to hit their pitch and if they walk you, so what!

For those of you on the fence with the opportunity to play for either a Division I program or a large Division II school, if you feel you can handle the Division I level, then go for it.

Also remember how scouts view the different levels. Take my story, for instance, and how I technically did worse offensively at a lower level in high school. Fortunately, I had already committed to Liberty University before the season, so it didn't matter.

Remember, scouts will most likely view the equation differently and assume a .548 average at a weaker program will transfer to around a .448 average at a much stronger program. This wasn't the case for me, yet this may be the case for some players.

Many solid Division II or Division III players get lost in the mix because scouts assume they wouldn't be able to handle the pro level, even though they might very well have been able to do so. Don't become the victim of that process: If you have a chance to play in a higher division, take it.

Whatever level you decide upon, make sure it is a legitimate opportunity. If there are players in front of you, be sure to factor in playing time or lack thereof, make your decision accordingly, and don't look back. If a Division II or Division III school has a solid program and you like the school and what it has to offer academically, then of course, factor that in as well. Maybe that is the best option for you. Weigh it all out and take that leap of faith. If you are still undecided, then ask your coach or a pro instructor in your area for more advice and what they feel is the best fit for you.

CHAPTER 10
TOP 10 BEST COLLEGE SUMMER LEAGUES

Don't let the fear of striking out hold you back.
—Babe Ruth

laying in a college summer league can be an invaluable experience, as it provides an opportunity for your talent to be on display alongside the top college players in the country. But before you decide to play summer ball, do your research—each league has its own characteristics and reputation.

While still a recruit in high school, this should be one of the questions you ask your future coaching staff when you are visiting your intended school: What college summer teams do the majority of your players compete for and does that vary depending upon the age of the players?

Sometimes, coaches will only promote their juniors (soon to be seniors) to the best summer leagues for fear of their players getting drafted after a stellar sophomore summer. Keep an eye out for that and trust your instincts. Also, while you're still in high school, ask the current players who are at that particular college you are interested in attending, whether they have received genuine opportunities to play summer ball, or if they were given empty promises. College summer ball is a sacrifice of your summer break, yet worth your while to get connected with pro scouts. College coaches usually coordinate their players' participation in summer ball, and they make arrangements before the spring season even gets underway. If your college coach is not well respected or doesn't have many contacts, then chances are you will have a hard time landing a spot with a competitive summer program.

Just as scouts view your skills differently based on what division your college team plays in, they view each summer league differently. I will go so far as to say that summer ball, if you are in one of the top 10 leagues, is more important than your college season for four reasons:

1. It shows your dedication to baseball throughout the whole year.
2. You are using a wood bat in the college summer league and showing your results based on wood and not metal.
3. All of the best college players in the nation are loaded into the top 10 summer leagues.
4. It gives scouts the opportunity to view many talented players all in one shot.

So which are the best leagues in the country?

These are the top 10 best summer leagues in the country based on how many players advance to the next level and the competition level of those that compete in these leagues:

10. **Perfect Game Collegiate League**—Located in the Northeast (mostly in upstate New York), Perfect Game is a compilation of teams and/or stadiums from the New York Collegiate Baseball League (NYCBL) that were bought out. Teams were added and took on a new name with the new owners. Perfect Game has

its roots as a a legit scouting service based out of Georgia and Florida that aids players in getting to the next level.

The Just Experience

I played in the NYCBL my freshman summer season. I remember two things about this league. I lived with a host mom who had a Hell's Angel tattooed on her forearm, in a trailer, with rusted silverware and rusted pots. My parents paid a visit and decided to buy her new pots, pans, and silverware and told me, "Good luck and keep chasing the dream!" Halfway through the season I ended up moving into another house to sleep on an authentic horsehair mattress that bowed like a "U." I tried turning it over and there were hundreds of spiders nesting in the horsehair. The floor was my best bet after that. Secondly, I never saw mosquitoes this big until I saw the movie *Mosquito*. YouTube "eye-popping scene from movie *Mosquito*" if you want to get a better idea. Other than my horrendous experience back in 2003, I'm sure the league is now lovely since Perfect Game is involved. Nevertheless, bring mosquito repellent just in case!

---

9. **Futures Collegiate League**—Run by former pros with proven résumés and connections, it has taken some teams that the New England League has passed on and developed into a solid college summer program. This league is comprised of teams located in Massachusetts, Connecticut, and New Hampshire.

8. **West Coast League**—Known for its awesome scenery, this league with teams in British Columbia, Washington, and Oregon

has attracted a ton of scouts and solid competition. The West Coast League now ranks higher than the once highly ranked Alaska League. This league is mostly fed from West Coast programs and provides another avenue for this area of the country to gain notoriety.

7. **Prospect League**—It's hard to find a summer league where you get to play in former pro stadiums consistently. The Prospect League from the Midwest was formed from former Frontier League Independent pro teams and merged with the former Central Illinois Collegiate League (CICL). The first league I signed into was the Frontier League, and some of those stadiums are gorgeous. The Prospect League is a solid league that gives you great exposure in the central United States, and it makes the most sense for those already going to college in this area.

6. **Valley League**—According to the Valley League website (www.valleyleaguebaseball.com/view/valleyleaguebaseball/directory-5/league-history-10), "The VBL is funded in part by a grant from Major League Baseball and is a member of the National Alliance of College Summer Baseball, a national affiliation of 13 collegiate summer leagues. The Valley League has produced well over 1,100 professional baseball players, including a record 79 former players drafted in the 2008 Major League Baseball First-Year Player Draft. In 2015, 30 Valley League alumni were playing in the Major Leagues and 15 alumni were either playing or serving in a [sic] executive capacity in 2014 with one of the MLB Post Season teams. In 2015, 46 current players or alumni were drafted." The Valley League has been running since 1961.

5. **Coastal Plains League**—Located in Virginia, North Carolina, and South Carolina, it's an old league with much history and class. It is basically the Cape Cod League of the Southeast. It was founded in 1937 and is still going strong today. It has an abundance of scouts in attendance and provides a high level of summer ball competition.

4. **Texas Collegiate League**—An opportunity to get exposure from one of the top states in the MLB draft year after year. This league plays throughout the state of Texas and has churned up a lot of positive noise since 2003. Many scouts are down this way and, if you attend schools in any surrounding states and have the opportunity to play here and attract attention, then it's a no-brainer if you are granted the opportunity.

3. **Northwoods Baseball League**—They have the cap on the north central United States, and the league includes a team in Canada too. This league has the most fan support of any summer league. With 18 teams, there's something special happening here. Many solid MLB guys came out of this league and continue to do so. If you are located in other parts of the country for college and you get the opportunity to play in it, you should highly consider it. They run an amazingly solid league.

2. **New England Collegiate Baseball League**—They do a great job of getting players exposure, and if it weren't for the Cape Cod League, they would be the premier league in the country. I played for the Torrington Twisters in this league and we played Team USA, Team Italy, and many other surprise teams along the course of our season. Many players were drafted out of this league. They feel they are competitive with the Cape Cod

League, but I would disagree . . . they're a very close second. It's close due to its proximity to the best league in the nation; scouts can make a short drive and catch a large talent pool from both leagues.

1. **Cape Cod League**—The Cape (as it is commonly known) is in New England, and is the oldest league, dating back to 1885. It has excellent fan support, and many scouts in attendance: Scouts consider it the *best of the best of the best*. The league has solid players, but it also has the hype. I've played with guys who have played in the Cape and hit around .250 and every scout wanted that player. ".250 in the Cape is like batting .900 anywhere else!"

Okay, that's an exaggeration, but the scouts view all of these players as cream of the crop if they can just somewhat hold their own. This is why if you have even the most remote chance of playing in the Cape, you must try to capitalize on it. The Cape Cod League is your goal by the time you are a college junior if you can perform at this level. If you aren't sure if you're Cape caliber, then ask yourself this question: "Are you a top 10 hitter or pitcher in your conference and is your conference a top Division I conference?" If so, then you could have a solid chance to perform here if you maintain your confidence and work ethic. If your college coach has a connection with any coach in this league or he is the coach himself, then that, of course, will help you land a contract with the Cape.

Any of the top 10 summer leagues mentioned will increase your chances if you perform. There are other highly credible leagues as well that are not mentioned above, such as the Alaska League, Atlantic Collegiate League, Florida Collegiate, Hamptons Collegiate, M.I.N.K Collegiate League, Great Lakes

League, and California Collegiate League. Keep in mind, you have to be cautious and thoroughly think your decision through when you sign with a summer team, no matter which league you choose. Summer teams contract you usually through the connections of your college head coach, and it's a strict contract with generally no exit clause other than signing professionally.

For example, I was signed on with the NECBL's Torrington Twisters and halfway through the season the Cape Cod League became interested in me. The Cape had me on their reserve list before the start of the summer season in case one of their players was hurt or signed professionally. When the Cape called for me, the Twisters management involved told them I was under contract and they wouldn't let me out of it. I didn't learn about the call until after the season.

I have a client who played in the Coastal Plains League for a season, performed well, and was reissued a contract the following year. Two weeks after he signed it, the Cape Cod League called and asked him if he was available to sign on with them. My friend begged and pleaded with the Coastal Plains commissioner and the team manager to let him out of his contract, and both the manager and commissioner gave him the following lip service: "You will get just as noticed in our league as you will in the Cape." It was a partial truth, because yes, he would still get noticed because the Coastal Plains is a highly credible league, but if he had played in the Cape and performed well, it would have helped his chances so much more since it is considered the best summer league with the largest talent pool. I also understand why the Coastal Plains did what they did, and quite frankly it's not a shocker. They have contracts for a reason and have to protect their players from constantly jumping ship anytime there's an opening in the Cape or anywhere else the player may prefer. Be aware of all of this when you sign your summer contract and make sure it's truly your best opportunity, but keep in mind that summer ball, no matter what league, could significantly improve your chances of playing pro ball if you perform well.

CHAPTER 11
THE PROS

The choices we make lead up to actual experiences. It is one thing to decide to climb a mountain. It is quite another to be on top of it.
—Herbert A. Simon

What is the difference between an advisor and an agent and are they necessary? How does the MLB draft work and what factors influence which players are drafted? Understanding the draft will allow you to more objectively assess your options. The player's personal circumstances, the team making the offer, and other opportunities for the player are some of the considerations that need to be thought through, even for a high school player who has caught the attention of the pros. How does playing Independent ball impact the player and future opportunities? Independent ball is professional baseball, yet it is not sanctioned by Major League Baseball. Understanding the positives and negatives of Independent leagues can help you make better decisions about whether or not you should pursue this path.

An Advisor or Agent?

Having an agent is illegal for high school and college players. However, an advisor is not. So what's the difference? An agent is an advisor before he can legally become an agent, which is after a pro team has officially signed or drafted you. But according to NCAA rules, "An athlete is ineligible if he agrees in any way, shape or form to be represented by an agent. This rule applies even if the player agrees to wait until after signing his professional contract before paying the agent."

A common situation is if you are having a great year and you end up conversing with an advisor along the way, which is not illegal unless you are paying him or he is gifting you or fighting for you with other teams. You have to make sure the advisor is smart and will abide by the rules of the NCAA.

Here is the definition of an agent and advisor from the NCAA:

Council broadens 'agent' definition*
NCAA.com
Last Updated—Jan 12, 2012 12:29 EST

INDIANAPOLIS—The Division I Legislative Council tabled several proposals in anticipation of the work of the Transforming Intercollegiate Athletics: Rules Working Group's recommendations later this year, though it did cast votes Wednesday on several key pieces of legislation.

Council chair Carolyn Campbell-McGovern, senior associate executive director of the Ivy League, said the meeting was different than a customary Council meeting because members didn't pore over every detail of each proposal.

"We tabled a significant number of proposals in deference to the fact that there are a lot of discussions going on about what our rules need to look like," Campbell-McGovern said.

However, the Council approved a rule that broadens the definition of agents to include third-party influences, including family members, who market student-athletes' athletics ability or reputation for personal financial gain. The rule, sponsored by the Amateurism Cabinet, would include individuals who either directly or indirectly:

- Represent or attempt to represent a prospective or current student-athlete in the marketing of his or her athletics ability or reputation for financial gain; or
- Seek to obtain any type of financial gain or benefit from securing a prospect's enrollment at an institution or a student-athlete's potential earnings as a professional athlete.

The new definition would include certified contract advisors, financial advisors, marketing representatives, brand managers or anyone who is employed by or associated with such individuals.

Campbell-McGovern said the new rule was in line with the division's principles and simply "closed a loophole."

In the past, the agent definition applied generally to third parties marketing an athlete's skills to a professional sports team. The new rule expands the definition to include people, including parents, marketing athletics skills to a collegiate institution for personal gain.

The rule is not intended to capture parents or legal guardians, athletics department staff members, former teammates or those individuals who have the best interests of a prospective student-athlete or student-athlete in mind from assisting or providing information to a prospective or enrolled student-athlete, provided they do not intend to receive a financial gain for their assistance.

---

* Reprinted with the permission of the National Collegiate Athletic Association.

Your advisor should not be present during any contract offer discussions or have any contact with that team. The advisor will know some scouts, so he will be careful not to mention your name when he isn't supposed to.

If a player's advisor is known to push the envelope and violate certain rules, then it could be held against you. The advisor could also be considered an agent, thereby jeopardizing your eligibility. So you need to converse with a smart advisor who has contacts in the scouting world, and is wise enough to not go beyond his network. Life is all about connections, so use them, but definitely use them wisely.

There are plenty of agents scoping ball fields that will waste your time. I had three to be exact. One I would consider an advisor; he stayed in touch with me hoping I would be drafted high and, as soon as I wasn't drafted at all, he never returned my call again. The other two were agents or "wannabe" agents who latched on to me after I was signed in Indy ball. Those two agents never had any powerful contacts or any clientele who made it to the big leagues. They figured they had nothing to lose by giving me a call and I figured the same. I was promised a gym to train at and a field to play on, and neither one was there for me.

The Just Experience

One time I was invited to stay at my agent's dad's house in Florida. I was without a vehicle, getting yelled at constantly, and was forced to work his dad's flea market stand. I remember waking up and no one was around for hours; there was no food in the house and I was without a car. Since I was in Florida, I walked to his neighbor's yard and snagged some grapefruits off of a tree for breakfast and lunch and said to myself, "I love Florida and all, but what the #*%$# am I doing here?"

Ask how many prospects the agent has taken on and how many are in the major leagues today. If he has at least a few and is a solid operation, and you can independently verify that those players were genuinely his clients, then it sounds worth having him in your corner to represent you during (as your advisor) and after (as your agent) the draft. If he stammers in response to the question or can't answer it directly, proceed in the conversation with the following: "Thank you for your interest in me as a player. I will have to get back to you. Have a splendid day." Click. After you have signed professionally and you land a solid agent, he, for the most part, passes the baton over to the scout who signed you, to help provide stability in that organization. The scout will then help fight for you somewhat in the winter meetings and a good agent will be in touch with you to give advice on your future and options you have along the way. Agents also provide contracts with certain merchandise for you to wear and play with at no cost to you. Agents take a percentage of your major-league contract, assuming you sign one, and they do everything they can to help get you there. The right agent or advisor can be a worthwhile investment for your future. Make sure you do the research.

The MLB Draft

Everyone who dreams of playing Major League Baseball plays the scenario over and over again in his mind of getting picked in the draft. It's a rite of passage and an accomplishment for all the hard work and dedication that a player has put into the sport. It is without a doubt a résumé builder.

The Just Experience

A neighbor once played a cruel joke on me. It was the summer of freshman year of high school when I received a call from an unknown number to my cell. The caller said, "Is Mike Just there please?"

I said, "Yes, I'm Mike, what's up?"

"This is Joe from the New York Yankees calling and we have taken an interest in you as a player."

I jumped straight up from my seat, spilled my drink and then "Joe" on the other end laughed and said, "Haha I'm just kidding . . . hey man it's Mike your neighbor."

"Oh, come on Mike!" (I could have killed him. . . .)

The draft or signee phone call is a surreal moment and one I wish everyone could achieve. Mine came as a free agent signee when I was on a trip to Disney World in December 2007. I was with my wife, sister, and sister's friend when the Houston Astros called. We popped open a bottle of champagne as we were dining at a fancy restaurant in Downtown Disney. How apropos!

"The draft is a funny thing," Tim Teufel said to my father when I was playing for Liberty University with his son Shawn Teufel. "Sometimes things go as planned and sometimes things get crazy in those meetings."

My friend Phil Laurent was told by the Chicago White Sox scout the day of the draft that he was to expect a call in the 8th round. Phil called me all excited and informed me about it. I told him I wished him all the best and of course I meant it. Unfortunately, no one called Phil that day or the next and he went undrafted entirely.

Mike receives the call from the Houston Astros while in Disney, just a few short miles away from the team's spring training complex. *Photo courtesy of Danielle Just.*

An Oakland A's scout also told me, "Those drafts get crazy and you never know what's going to happen until it happens." Sounds similar to what Tim Teufel said!

You can't get mad at the scout. He probably liked Phil, but got overruled in the meeting. Sometimes the draft can appear political. "Drafted 10th overall is Donny Baseball, Son of Father Roger Baseball. Next up is Joe Shmo (third cousin twice removed from Ty Cobb). Congrats! You're the next contestant on *The Price Is Right . . . come on down*! And Joe has *no legs*! But *that's okay* because he has a solid upper torso profile. We will teach him how to run. Give him a mil."

Knowing people in the industry is important. If you have a connection, it would be best to use it.

So what if you don't have any connections?

How do you get there, what should you know, and when should you sign?

Whether you should sign or not in the draft has to be evaluated based on each individual's circumstances. There are many variables to consider such as:

- Age of the player drafted;
- Eligibility remaining;
- Other offers from colleges or potential pro teams on the table;
- Evaluating each organization and its development;
- Players ahead of you per position and their production;
- The scout that drafted you and his impact on the organization;
- Your agent's take on the situation . . . and many more.

So, you need to do your homework and be prepared while having a good attorney in place.

Some things to also research are:

- What did each organization pay each player in each round last year? Chart it or pull it up online. Have an idea what your value is based on previous signees.
- Did the three players drafted before you sign? If yes, and they are all lefty pitchers as are you, then guess what, if you don't take their offer then they may not care. However, if all three lefty pitchers decline, then not only do they want you badly now but they have more money laying around to sweeten the pie, since the other three opted not to sign.

This is why, in some instances, it's important to sign quickly and, in other cases, it's important to drag your feet to see what the others decide to do. Each circumstance is unique, so do your research.

If you are signed with a decent bonus of say $100,000 or more, then odds are the organization is willing to invest more time to allow you to develop as well.

Tip!

Signing bonuses vary depending upon the organization and what it considers a higher prized value per round in accordance with the age, projection, and position of the player. For example, in 2016 the 24th pick overall of the draft went to San Diego who signed a player for 1 million, but the Chicago White Sox had a later pick as the 26th overall player of the draft and signed him for little over 2 million.

Some organizations pay millions more than others. The more money they are willing to pay you, usually the longer they are willing to keep you around. The money is nice to have as an incentive; however, it is also your security in that organization. Richard Branson, founder of Virgin Group, had a famous quote: "If someone offers you an amazing opportunity and you're not sure you can do it, say yes—then learn how to do it later."

Tip!

Don't let fear become a reason
to turn down an opportunity.
Also don't let pride get in the way
of your opportunity.

If an organization is offering you something, it may be the only time it gets offered. Make sure you thoroughly weigh your decision and seek guidance from outsiders' perspectives before you decline an offer. Two final questions to consider:

Will you have potential for more opportunities?

What if you are signed as a free agent with little or no bonus?

After the 15th round or so, bonuses can be nonexistent or rare, depending upon the age of the player and his eligibility. If you find yourself in that position, it's a tough decision, because you won't carry that much weight in an organization without any of their money invested in you. It doesn't mean you can't move up the professional ladder, but it will be a harder climb than the guy who has their investment money. But it's still important to take advantage of every opportunity, so you may decide to sign under this circumstance and hope for the best.

Independent Ball—Good or Bad Move?

Independent ball is hard to get into. Though some people call it "semipro," it is not—it is still paid-to-play professional baseball, yet it is not sanctioned by Major League Baseball. You usually need a scout's recommendation or pro experience to have an opportunity to play, but others can break in too. The way players usually get signed back into affiliated ball from Independent ball is to have an agent or scout who still has their best interests in mind. It does happen, but rarely will a player get picked up out of this league on a whim.

One would hope your Independent ball manager's job, in addition to running the team, is to help push you back into affiliated ball, which is your ultimate goal. But does your goal align with your manager's goal? What manager in any Indy league would actively make calls on your behalf and say, "Here you go! Please take my five best players!?" That doesn't make sense, does it? Why would the manager want to lose his best players and potentially end up with an atrocious win/loss record to help the players advance? Wouldn't the manager rather build his résumé to further his managerial career? If the manager prioritizes the players' careers over the team's success, there's a chance the GM will not renew the manager's contract the following year because the fan support will decline when losses build up. Losses then have a snowball effect, which results in poor attendance and slower concession sales.

Not all Independent teams and leagues are like this, but you need to understand the circumstances they have to deal with in every league; sometimes you have to be a little pushy with your Independent manager, without showing disrespect, if you want an opportunity with an affiliated baseball team after producing in Independent baseball.

Pay in all Independent leagues depends upon your rank as a player. The veterans get paid the most. Then there's LS5, LS4, LS3, LS2, LS1, Rookie. There are different Independent leagues across the country. Here are a few of the most popular:

The Frontier League

In the 1990s the Frontier League was more of a beginner pro league, but that is no longer the case. The league continues to be on the rise, providing larger pro talent pools and transactions to affiliated professional organizations. However the maximum player salary is only $1,600 a month.

Mike Just in one of his first pro games running out to his position with a young player to salute the flag for our National Anthem. *Photo courtesy of Don Adams Jr.*

The Just Experience

When I was a rookie in the Frontier League, my salary of a whopping $600 a month was almost enough for both the peanut butter and the jelly.

Most players that are released out of Rookie ball or A ball try to play in this league.

There is also an age cap in the league of 27. The league is good for players who continue to perform and have agents continuing to make calls for them, and there are scouts on the prowl who are willing to take a chance on a player at this level.

After I played a season here, I referred my friend Phil Laurent from Liberty to my manager and he said, "Funny you should mention him because Phil's name was in the mix already. What is Phil like?" So I sold Phil hard to my manager and he sent him a contract soon thereafter.

The competition in the Frontier League plays similar to Rookie ball or Low A. If you are just blending in here, not standing out, and have no agent calling affiliated pro teams on your behalf, then eventually you will either get released, or end your Frontier League career when you hit the age limit.

Northern League or American Association and Can-Am

Mike being interviewed before the start of a game, and signing autographs for fans. *Photos courtesy of Mike and Linda Jones.*

The Northern League has disbanded and merged with the American Association League. They also play interleague games against the Can-Am League, which has a similar level of competition. Many formerly affiliated Double A guys play in this league and the competition is comparable to a High A or soft Double A league. The pay is more than the Frontier League, but not much more. The pay starts at $800.

The Just Experience

In 2007, I was getting paid $1,000 a month in the Northern League. Woo Hoo! Nothing like getting paid below minimum wage and being pumped about it! But in a sense, when you're chasing a dream, $1,000 is a bonus.

Players who were producing were moving in and out of this league, but the key is how. The players that were getting signed were guys whose agents were working out deals with different organizations, or guys that were just in Triple A doing well and major-league teams couldn't find room for them on their rosters. So they sign an Indy ball contract in the meantime until the agent can work around the clock to try to get them another opportunity back in affiliated ball. A guy in my shoes, who didn't have a solid agent or any money invested in him with any organizations previously, or any scouts tied to him still trying to pull some strings, stood little chance to get into affiliated ball. A coach who has your back and has a proven track record of players in the past would be your best bet here.

The Just Experience

Here's how I got my opportunity with Houston. To put it bluntly, I basically shook down my manager in Fargo. After the season I had with the Fargo-Moorhead RedHawks, and after reviewing the history of that team and the statistics from previous seasons, I realized my stats were almost comparable to Roger Maris's stats when he played in that league. I told myself, *something needs to happen here.*

My manager said, "Next year I want you to be my everyday second baseman again."

I replied, "Hold it right there. If I don't get a contract from an affiliated organization then there won't be a next year. I want my shot and I feel I deserve it." It's a poker match and I played a bold hand. My manager then left me a voicemail an hour later and said, "Here's your shot. Good luck and Merry Christmas."

A week later, the Houston Astros called with news they had purchased my contract.

Amazing how influential some of these coaches are, but are they all willing to help you accomplish your goals? They all have different agendas. Was his sincere or not? I have no way of knowing. What I do know is he did come through with his connections and I truly enjoyed playing for him. The article below was released soon thereafter in the *Bergen Record*.

TBALL   THE RECORD **S-7**

e for the Rockies

clean more than two years, iving him to get his life in order and resume his career.

The Reds got him in the Rule 5 ft before last season. Hamilton s warmly received in Cincinti, where he readily shared his story and became a fan favorite. He was expendable because the Reds already have outfielders Ken Griffey Jr., Adam Dunn and Ryan Freel.

Volquez, a 24-year-old right-hander, was 2-1 with a 4.50 ERA in six starts for the Rangers last season and was considered one of their top pitching prospects. He was honored as their top minor league pitcher last season.

Astros snatch Just

HOUSTON — Second baseman Mike Just of Woodcliff Lake likely will enjoy his holiday a bit more after learning the Houston

Astros purchased his contract from the Fargo-Moorhead Red-Hawks of the Northern League.

Just, 24, was named the 2007 Northern League Rookie of the Year after coming over from the River City Rascals of the Frontier League during spring training.

Just, who starred at St. Joseph Regional, batted .336 with 24 doubles, four home runs, 55 RBI and 56 runs scored in 94 games this year. He posted a .420 on-base percentage and stole a team-leading 20 bases.

Just also led Northern League second baseman in fielding percentage at .990, making only five errors.

"He did a great job for us in 2007 and was a major part of our success," RedHawks manager Doug Simunic said. "The Astros are getting a good, hard-nosed ballplayer who can do a lot of

positive things on the field."

Watson denies link

NEW YORK - A day after being linked to drugs in baseball, former pitcher Allen Watson denied the allegation.

Watson was among nine players accused of doping by former pitcher Jason Grimsley in a federal agent's affidavit unsealed Thursday.

"I at no time over my professional baseball career used steroids or any performance-enhancing drugs. Not then, not now, not ever," Watson said in a statement released by his agent, Tony Giordano.

Watson, 37, was 51-55 with a 5.03 ERA from 1993-2000. The lefty pitched for St. Louis, San Francisco, the Los Angeles Angels, the Mets, Seattle and the Yankees.

Atlantic League

Mike signing autographs for kids. *Photo courtesy of Joseph Novak/JCN Digital Photography.*

What the Cape is to college summer leagues, the Atlantic League is to Indy ball.

It's the "crème de la crème," "the Best of the Best."

Many players dream of playing here, and few do. The salaries are decently high for minor-league ball. I made $1,600 a month and they paid for my gas too, since I was fortunate enough to commute from home. Some guys make thousands more than that, and I've heard stories in every Indy league of paying some guys extra under the table to maintain the team's salary cap. I may or may not have been one of them with the Newark Bears before they folded. This league is for elite players only and is best suited for them. Their agents are working around the clock to get them back into affiliated ball, and there's so much back and forth from affiliated to Atlantic throughout one season that you can't even keep track of it all. In 2009, we lost half of our team to either Mexico, affiliated pro ball, Taiwan, Japan, or some other pro league that paid more money.

The Atlantic League is an opportunity to play among former big leaguers who for whatever reason aren't currently in the majors. Sometimes it's not because they don't have it anymore. Maybe there was a steroid issue from the past, or an altercation that black-balled that player, or something illegal they got caught doing and were subsequently released. Maybe they have no story and were just flat out overlooked. Whatever the case, they are now in the Atlantic League and performing just as if they were playing in affiliated ball. The competition is comparable to Triple A and players move back and forth quite often.

The problem with this league is that it has such good competition that it's rare to stand out. No one stands out among a plethora of major leaguers except for one or two players who were former elite major leaguers. If you aren't a major leaguer and you are in the Atlantic League, chances are that you will blend in at best and, if you do, then how can you advance?

It looks much better to a scout if you're hitting .336 in the Northern League than .275 in the Atlantic League. Those were my numbers because of the increase in competition level, but without a scout or agent gunning for me, it wasn't possible for me to get out of there on my own and I wasn't going to lead the Atlantic League.

That's what the Northern League manager implied when he told me in our last phone call after I left his Northern League to join the Atlantic League. He said, "You will die in that league." He was mostly bitter I didn't re-sign with him, but it was an honest conversation where he wasn't entirely wrong. However, for a major leaguer, playing in this league can act as a "holding tank" for him until his agent moves him to a better-affiliated organization.

Indy Ball: Much Better Than Jail

Every player in Indy ball is there for a reason. They all have a story to tell. It's like jail in a way. "Don't you know everybody is innocent in here?" says that guy from *The Shawshank Redemption*. Same concept in Indy ball, only the stories in this case are true.

The league is like a conduit to a better place that everyone wants to get into. And the way each player got into Indy ball is as unique as each player's stance at the plate—someone was a victim of politics, made a dumb decision, or didn't get his shot for whatever reason and was trying to get back in to stand a fighting chance. Someone didn't know when to "hang 'em up" because they had been so close in Triple A, knocking on the door for seven years, and then they got released.

Baseball is all they knew, so they've become "institutionalized" to Indy ball, just like the prisoners at Shawshank. You're pushing 40 years old, your parents are still paying for your health care and gas, you have six icepacks on your arms and legs, with bruises everywhere, no college degree, no wife (or one barely hanging on), maybe a kid or two . . . but baseball is all they knew. Players who try to tell their sob stories in the locker room are frowned upon, because everyone has one. The guy that starts talking about it will clear out a locker room within seconds.

Nobody cares.

Everyone has a story.

The system isn't fair, the politics aren't fair, but wait . . . life isn't fair?

Baseball is the best preparation for life there is.

For me, learning the word *failure* through the game of baseball took me to a whole new level of growth as a young man. Isn't that a solid preparation for the perils that life throws at you? It takes the "baseball is life" quote to a whole different level. So think positive, engage your faith, and work hard and believe in your dream.

Some players get to the point in their careers where they have to learn to walk away from the game or someone will eventually turn them away.

The reality is that Indy ball is an incredible experience and an alternate route to playing pro ball, while still trying to make it to affiliated ball. Whether you were released from an affiliated team, or finished your college or Ju-Co season and are looking to play on and don't have anything else going, the Indy ball realm is worth it.

Obviously, a scout recommendation is big, but the different leagues do host tryouts as well and most are legitimate. Look into them and find out how many guys they sign from which tryouts.

Also, don't be afraid to speak up. If you have some leverage, tell the manager what you want and put it in the contract. For example, tell him you will commit to a season, but if you do a, b, c, and d, then he needs to do a, b, c, and d.

There's never a guarantee they can get you signed into affiliated ball, and if you get a guarantee such as that, then I would proceed cautiously and investigate further. But if you can find out who your manager or GM's connections are and how you can utilize them to your advantage during or after the season, then at least you're not letting them think that you are comfortable just playing for them, or that you will stay quiet so they can get three years out of you and then look to find your replacement. Speak up or forever hold your piece in Indy ball.

I wrote the following shortly after my retirement in 2009 after my long quest in Independent pro baseball:

"I took the road less traveled by . . . and Indy ball just wasn't where it's at."

That statement provided comic relief at the end of an era for me, but is not entirely true. I value the friends I met along the way, their stories and the memories we created, the many locations I've been to in and out of the country, the things I've learned about people's way of life all over the world, and the accolades I received. I also met some of the same major leaguers and major-league coaches I watched growing up as a child on TV (and played with in video games); I never dreamed that years later, I would be sitting next to them in dugouts, games, or practices such as: Gary Carter, Sid Bream, Jack Clark, Andy Van Slyke, Randy Tomlin, Armando Benitez, Keith Foulke, Edgardo Alfonzo, Jim Pankovits, Jeff Bagwell, Carl Everett, Pete Rose Jr., Jay Gibbons, Von Hayes, Chris Hoiles, Ramiro Mendoza, or meet and have opportunities to learn from my dad's heroes like Bud Harrelson, Brooks Robinson (who told me I played a heck of a third base), Maury Wills (who told me I was one hell of a baseball player and one of his favorites), Joe Ferguson (who signed a ball saying I was his favorite player to watch), Bobby Richardson, Butch Hobson (who signed a ball, "I love you man!"), Earl Weaver, Andy Etchebarren, Tommy John, Sparky Lyle, and so many more while learning from the best while getting paid to do it. My time in Independent ball also jumpstarted my future, giving me a better business sense and a more objective perspective on life.

I have nothing to complain about, yet everything to be thankful for.

Do I still have opportunities to play and could I still play? Absolutely. But I don't want to sit with icepacks on my elbows and knees, all bruised up with no income, no wife, and my future in doubt. I want to be able to retire at a young-enough age, and in order to do that, I needed to turn the page and focus my drive and determination elsewhere.

Somewhere the work ethic you put in gets reflected in return: the "reap what you sow" principle.

I once heard a coach say, "No one is ever content with their career, big league or not. They never want it to end." Why that's significant is because most people are not "lucky" enough to walk away. Someone else closes the door for them and their last game just had been. So sometimes if you're "lucky" everyone reluctantly walks away.

CHAPTER 12
WHY NOT YOU?

"All our dreams can come true if we have the courage to pursue them."
—Walt Disney

W*hy not me?* That's the question to ask yourself and firmly believe.

In baseball, players from all walks of life and all different backgrounds have an opportunity to chase their dreams.

Talent has no bias. All races, all backgrounds, all upbringings have a shot.

Therefore, you have a shot.

Keep in mind that less than 1 percent of players that play high school baseball will sign a pro contract.

If you never take a chance you will never know. Go for it! Why not you?

Just because you are doing it doesn't mean you are maximizing your production either. It's not enough to just show up and be a presence.

Actually try!

Actually work hard!

Actually hear, listen, and apply!

Be smart. Be coachable.

Choose wisely who you take advice from. Make sure they explain their actions thoroughly. If they don't, then politely ask questions.

Dream big! Envision yourself playing at a high level. Set goals so you have a plan of attack on how to get there.

Jerry Falwell Sr., the founder of Liberty University, explained vision on eight different levels. The four most applicable to baseball dreams are:

1. Vision is a bridge from the past to the future.
2. Vision is the eye of faith to see the invisible and the decisiveness to make it visible.
3. Vision is the inward fire which enables you to boldly communicate to your peers.
4. Vision is the God-given energy which will make you become a risk taker.

Are the best players in the major leagues you may ask? Yes and no.

How many Derek Jeters are there in the game today? How many players do you watch and say, wow he's a natural like Mike Trout, or had a personal connection like Mike Piazza to help his chances?

Sometimes a player becomes known as a "4A player." This term implies that he's a stud at the triple-A level, yet every time he gets a call-up he cannot produce. You may see a player struggling in the majors and have no idea he put up gargantuan numbers in Triple A the year prior.

Sometimes it's easier to hit in the majors, but not easier to get a hit. Umpires tend to be much more consistent in the major leagues, the lighting and visibility is better, the fields are immaculately groomed, and each major-league pitcher has impeccable command. All these factors can make you feel more secure in the box. Pitchers pound the strike zone (meaning they aren't afraid to throw the ball over the plate consistently and trust in their move-ment and velocity), and as a hitter at this level, you are aware of this. This doesn't mean you will always hit it, but it's comforting to know if the pitch was thrown at your head, at least you pretty much knew he meant it.

I've been told by a teammate that when Nolan Ryan used to throw to "Pudge" Rodriguez behind the dish, when certain rook-ies who were known phenoms from Triple A stepped into the box for the first time, they could count on seeing some nice chin music in the upper 90s. Pudge would then converse with the rookie and tell him something along these lines: "You know he meant that, and if he wanted to hit you, he would have. Welcome to the show. This is his plate just so you know." The intimidation factor, the movement, and the quickness of the fielders mean that even though major-league pitchers pound the strike zone, it can still be difficult for the "4A player" to produce in the majors.

I had a buddy, Matt Rizzotti, who was one of the backups for Ryan Howard at first for the Phillies, and he was eventually released. There was no need for him with Ryan there, and he wasn't versatile enough to move to another position. This hap-pens often, and if other organizations have money invested in other guys and have their rosters set, then even if they like a cer-tain player, their hands may be tied to make any moves to acquire him. It's the luck of the draw. Sometimes players have to retire or get hurt at the top in order for those at the bottom to even sniff a chance. I played with a top-round catcher who was released because another top prospect stole his bat. That prospect had scratched the catcher's name off the bat and scraped in his own. When the catcher confronted that prospect, and the prospect said he was keeping it, the catcher socked him in the face and the catcher was released the next day. Yes, he should have gone about it differently. However, he was the best receiving catcher I've ever played with and was never invited to set foot in affiliated ball again.

Randall Simon had the best footwork of any first baseman I've ever played with and hit .300 in the majors time and time again. He also happened to smack the hot dog person, who was racing between innings, with his bat as a joke. He didn't realize that it was a young girl in the costume and he knocked her down the stairs. She took it to the next level and Randall was never picked up again by any affiliated organization. I played with him with the Bears and he shared how he went above and beyond to help the girl and her family, but it was too late. He was out as the bad example.

Make wise choices, because the choices you make have long-term effects. Keep dreaming and working hard toward your dream. Your high school, club or travel team, college, and college summer ball coaches are all extremely important. They aid in your process of climbing the ladder. They set the stage for your career and may help return and make calls on your behalf. But remember that not all of them care to do that and some can even harm you, so choose your programs wisely!

The correct agent is important. He makes calls on your behalf.
The organization you're in is important.
The scout that shows interest in you is important.
The decisions you make and the work ethic you have is important.
Your grades are important.
How you profile per position is important.
Being at the right place at the right time is important.

You have the power to achieve only when you fully believe in yourself and have the work ethic to prove it. Russell Wilson, quarterback of the Seattle Seahawks, is known for quoting his father, who said, "Why not you Russ?" I'm saying the same to you . . . *so why not you?*

When Scott Brosius was in the minors, his coach told the team, "Statistically, only two of you are going to make it to the top." Scott looked around and wondered who the other player was going to be.

Like Scott, do have faith and believe in yourself and trust in your God-given ability to accomplish anything you set your mind to.

I wish you all the best in pursuit of your successful baseball career and hope this book will help you to better understand the industry, narrow your focus, prepare yourself for both the positives and negatives, and accomplish what you set out to achieve.

EXTRA BASES

A. Single—*Baseball Résumé Recruiting Video*

Hard work beats talent when talent doesn't work hard.
—Tim Notke (made popular by Kevin Durant)

In the game of baseball, a player has to prove himself no matter what was achieved the season before. Players are expected to match or exceed their numbers from the prior season. This does not change as you move up levels, and it's more important the higher you go.

As you work to match those high expectations year after year, a letter of recommendation or phone call from a reliable and trustworthy coach or instructor can provide some help along the sweat-infused journey.

I had a former coach write a letter, which I gave to my high school coach for some assurance and that helped my situation going into high school. Even if you are a recruit, it cannot hurt. There is such a thing as overkill when it comes to this, so don't go crazy having letters crafted, but one phone call or email from a highly regarded player or coach will only help alleviate some stress.

In baseball a résumé is not a piece of paper; it comes in the form of a recruiting video.

This video should include a slide in the beginning that pauses for roughly 10 seconds. For position players, the first slide will be slightly different than pitchers. If you are a "two-way" player (meaning you excel as both pitcher and hitter) then include that on the first slide. For position players it should contain your 60-yard time (standard metrics for speed) and 30-yard time (home to first), and cite by whom and where those times were recorded. If your dad recorded them, you may want to get a more objective source, such as a college camp or showcase, and then mention that on the slide. If the time was recorded via laser, then that should be mentioned as well, because laser time is generally the most accurate and usually records a tenth or two tenths slower than a stopwatch.

For both position players and pitchers, include as much of the following information as you can: your name, age, graduating class, address, primary position, secondary position, height, weight, personal email address, and personal cell phone; your parents' cell phones; your GPA and SAT or ACT score; whether you throw right or left, bat right or left or switch; your ball exit speed and arm strength velocity and where both were accurately tested; the school you currently attend, address of the school, and potential college major; your guidance counselor's name, email, and phone number; your high school coach's name, email, and phone number; your summer coach's name, email, and phone number; and a picture of yourself in uniform or game action shot. Any recent large accomplishments that set you apart such as "MVP of a tournament" should also be included on that first slide. If something stands out such as an average or ERA, then include that on the first slide as well. If you're wondering how a coach will read all of the above information in 10 seconds, the answer is that he won't. However, he will pause it and reflect on it before he continues to watch the video of your mechanics.

If showcasing yourself as a position player, you will need to show hitting, fielding, and throwing in the video. Speed is assumed from the first slide and your times recorded. The entire video should be roughly five minutes long. College coaches don't want to watch a movie of you and more than likely they won't watch all five minutes anyway. They most likely will see a few swings and skip around. For hitting, show a view from the catcher's perspective and also show a view from the side. The coach wants to see the flight and carry of the ball off the bat from behind, as well as the mechanics of your swing from the side. Tee work, soft toss, front toss, and overhand are all good options to include. This segment should be no longer than an edited two and a half minutes.

For infielders, show your footwork and approach to the ball on balls right at you, to your left and right, as well as a slow roller, and how quickly and accurately you throw to first. Also showcase your footwork around the bag at second if you're a middle infielder and your footwork around the bag at first if you're a first baseman. If you're an outfielder, show how you approach the ball and set your feet prior to catching it and show a crow hop (footwork designed specifically for outfielders to gain more momentum to throw with maximum exit speed) from a view behind looking toward the catcher, and a view from the catcher looking at you, but make sure the shot is close enough to see form. Pitchers should include their velocity on the front slide too. Also be sure to show views from the side for the college coach to assess proper mechanics, as well as from behind the pitcher to see the flight of the ball to the catcher. Show all pitches from side and back angle in your video as well.

B. Double—*The Long Toss Program*

*Long Toss. Far and away the most important drill
for strengthening my arm.*
—Phil Quantrill (former MLB pitcher
with impeccable power and command)

In addition to resistance bands to strengthen your rotator cuffs, incorporating a long toss program into your regimen will increase your arm strength, but only if your mechanics are correct. Training with bad mechanical habits can put strain on your arm and can lead to injury. Consult a knowledgeable coach or instructor to ensure you're utilizing your glove arm and lower half properly. Your proper release point will vary depending upon your body type and position.

Using a four-seam grip, start about 15 feet away (if 12 years old or younger, then about 12 feet away). For every three or four throws you make, take a couple of steps back and do it again until you have about 50–60 good throws in total. The distance goal should be 90–125 feet for players 13 and under and a minimum of 175 feet for a high school player. High school pitchers should strive for 6–10 throws per interval and a minimum distance of 200 feet. *Note*: Throwing more is *not* better; throwing through a disciplined program appropriate for age and position will see better improvement and results, if throwing mechanics are correct.

Apply the program twice a week to start. When you throw, your throws can have some arc to them the farther away you go, but make sure they don't have a large rainbow arc.

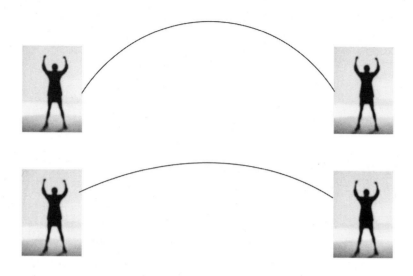

Assuming the distance is about 175 feet apart, the first example shows too much of an arc, thus stretching out different muscle groups and a release point that will not be used in a regular throwing motion in game situations. The second example is most accurate with some arc to it, but more of a straighter line. If you decide to throw from a longer distance, you may increase the arc slightly, but if you cannot reach your target on this arc, then it's better to one-hop your partner as opposed to increasing to a high arc.

It's better to work out muscle groups that you will be throwing with regularly in a game. If you are throwing sky-high popups because you're trying to reach your partner on a line from 300 feet away, then all you are doing is stretching out other muscles that you won't be using in a game. You want to practice how you will play and utilize the specific muscle groups to maximize performance and build muscle memory.

After you reach your peak distance, then start working your way back in with about 10 more throws. If you're an infielder, this is the time you can work a quick hands drill and incorporate quickness of feet as well from 40–50 feet away.

C. Triple—*Baseball Is Life*

Well, baseball was my whole life. Nothing's ever been as fun as baseball.
—Mickey Mantle

Sports is a wonderful catalyst upon which character can be forged and life lessons taught. Baseball is no exception. Baseball encourages discipline, perseverance, mental toughness, teamwork, selflessness, confidence, and numerous other traits that are critical for success in baseball, but even more so as players go on and pursue other careers, establish families, and make a difference in their communities.

The game is a worthy endeavor when it is pursued in the right way for the right reasons, can bring a kind of joy like no other, and has lasting benefits beyond one's baseball career.

It is often said on T-shirts or banners at stadiums—"baseball is life." The truth is considerably more complex than that simplistic phrase would imply. Baseball is a character builder and strengthens mental toughness.

What's the proper mindset during an injury? What is okay to play through and what is to be taken more seriously? How does this mental toughness carry into life? What if you have to perform a concert and you have a headache 20 minutes before the start of the show? Oh well! You better suck it up and get out there! What about when you are down 15 runs? How do you handle that situation? Do you mope around or do you show the same hustle? What about in the real world when you are late on a credit card payment due to lack of funds? Do you mope around and do nothing about it or do you find a way to scratch and claw, work overtime and ensure you get that payment in somehow, someway? Do you sacrifice time, pride, sleep, and who knows what else or do you just pack it in or hope it will figure itself out? I can tell you right now it won't just figure itself out on its own.

The hard work and mental toughness you learn in baseball will carry over into many aspects of life and will give you an edge over the non-athlete. Because baseball is a complex game, there are many life lessons you can learn that are applicable to life off the field.

You may find yourself coaching a team or conducting a one-on-one private lesson. There is so much opportunity to be a positive role model when baseball is your life.

D. Home Run—*Importance of a Coach/Instructor as a Mentor*

I'm a success today because I had a friend who believed in me and I didn't have the heart to let him down.
—Abraham Lincoln

My life is baseball, but my life is also about people—and a passion for helping them achieve all they can in the game I love. Athletes and instructors are held up on a pedestal and considered role models, especially by those students with whom they work regularly. While conducting a lesson, instructors must take extra precautions with the content they share and the example they set.

Mike invited his client Andrew to the Jersey Shore for more mentorship/bonding opportunities beyond baseball. Pictured left to right after Mike took Andrew clamming for the first time: Mike Just, Andrew Morel, Mike's friend Logan Thompson. *Photo courtesy of Mike Just.*

I have students who open up to me on many different levels. For me to be the best instructor I can be, I need to listen to what each player needs.

If my student is not confident, I discover why. It could be much more than a simple personality trait. Maybe he is feeling the pressure from his father bearing down on him. Maybe he is abused at home. Abuse has many forms and some players don't even realize they are succumbing to it. An issue as large as that could be the main hindrance, so if my job is to gain confidence from this particular player, I cannot do so unless I work with him on a solution, and then proceed with the adjustments to regain that confidence. Maybe I have to build that confidence from scratch, but, either way, we will be moving in the right direction at that point.

A great instructor needs to be able to dive into the psyche of the player and understand him on a personal level. This can also be very dangerous when you go there. If you don't allow the child to open up to you, then you will merely scratch the surface with that player. How will you ever know what that player was capable of unless you uproot the issues and let that player know he is not alone and you are there every step of the way to provide a solution and help him deal with the issue(s)? The instructor should not get too personal, unless the player opens up about it. If the player isn't swinging hard and his mood is down, then you shouldn't just pretend like you don't notice it. Stop the lesson, look the player in the eyes, and ask:

"What's wrong? This isn't like you and I know you very well. Tell me what's wrong and let me see how I can help you with what you're battling right now."

More often than not, the player will communicate to the instructor if enough trust is built up. I have had two players on two separate occasions mention a death in the family in that moment (which allowed me to at least be aware of what I was up against and how to comfort those players in that moment), or someone who was bullying them, or something small that I was able to squash in two seconds and get that player's mind right again. You can be persistent up to a point if the player won't tell you, but don't harass the player either if he's not ready to talk.

If you are training a player under the age of 18 and the parent is not present, be sure to mention any conversations you had with the player in private with the parent. You want to work with the parent on this and not against him/her. If the parent is the main issue, then maybe contact the other parent. If both parents are issues and it is very serious, then you may be obligated to contact authorities. Know the rules of your particular state and your responsibilities. If it is something you can handle, then breathe wisdom into the player and deal with him directly and build off of that.

You may be thinking, "Why would an instructor be concerned with all of these issues with the player when he is just paid to simply improve his game?"

How can his game be improved when other issues are clouding the player's mind? You won't accomplish much at all unless you address the issue head-on, and then you can move forward. There are times where I have to take the player out of the cage and sit him down privately on the side during his lesson. Sometimes the change of scenery or privacy allows that player to really open up on a totally different level, and then you can build trust, and from there accomplish great things with that player on a much deeper level. Once again, if you have to give a negative answer, be sure to use the "sandwich approach" and include some positive as well.

Make sure your responses are well articulated, and make sure you are steering that player in the right direction by working toward some conclusion. If you are in over your head, then inform the parents. The player is relying on you for those answers, and this could be a pivotal moment in his life, so do your best not to let him down.

A good mentor is hard to find, and not every instructor is up to the task. I know of many instructors who lead countless players astray in many ways. Most of the time it's easy to blame the parents for allowing their children to be under the influence of such condescending coaching. It's not okay just because you think that your son will have an advantage going into high school, or their swing may improve. If you are in high school and that coach is a bad apple, and baseball is in your child's future, then leave! Stop basing your decisions on the program and how great it is, as opposed to how great a mentor that coach is for you. At what cost and what sacrifice are you willing to attempt to improve your game?

If a player gets indoctrinated with mountains of pride, self-loathing, sexual references, or other inappropriate behavior over the course of four years of high school, those will be hard habits to break down the road. If that's the cost, was improving his game even worth it?

When kids watch baseball on television, they are exposed to tobacco use, speculation about steroid use, lies, cursing, egos, and promiscuity. These players are the role models for our youth, and something needs to change. Baseball players seem to have some sort of free pass to be horrible examples and freely use "locker room talk," and that's just the norm in the industry. But that doesn't mean I have to allow my son to succumb to it.

In our facility we strive to *change the perspective of the pro baseball player while changing players' lives for the better.* This starts with the attitude change on the part of the instructor. When that instructor starts to lead by a positive example, then he sets the bar high for the rest of the staff as well as the players with whom he trains. Obviously the teaching and training methods an instructor uses are important in the physical development of the player, but how are you developing that player's mind and massaging his brain? Just because you can teach the perfect top hand regarding the swing doesn't mean the player's mindset will be in the right place to perform that adjustment come game time anyway.

A solid instructor will build the whole package. For a player to become the best all-around athlete and person he can be, he must be trained mentally, physically, and emotionally so he can understand baseball from all perspectives. Most coaches just train one dimension and some dabble in two. It's the three-dimensional coaches that make the best mentors. Seek out these coaches/instructors.

Each parent and player coming in for lessons will have different goals in mind. I've had parents tell me, "My kid isn't making it to the major leagues, so why waste the money on private lessons?" This parent whose kid is 10 is thinking way too big picture and not taking into consideration the moment at hand. I'm not suggesting their statement is false, because the odds are against the player. However, what if that player doesn't socialize well or have many friends in school? What if he is learning how to be competitive and work better in teams? What if that player, who never hit the ball and always got made fun of by his teammates, can now learn to hit and enjoy the moment of his first hit? Maybe that player will make a friend or two because of it.

Maybe he ends up becoming better than expected and ends up positioning himself in a leadership role on the team. Maybe he's the captain one day or he gets the game-winning hit! Then, was the lesson worth it? It certainly was, especially if that player is learning confidence and how hard work can achieve small doses of success, which in turn is a great life lesson.

Other players and parents have higher ambitions, and proper instruction may increase the chances of a college scholarship. When a positive instructor is willing to sacrifice himself for the player, an unbreakable mentor/athlete bond can form.

I have had players call me when they had a problem in school, or at their friend's house, and they didn't know what to do. Sometimes situations become awkward for that player to share with the parents, so who else is next in line who they feel most comfortable with? Once again, if you are an instructor who truly cares, and players come to you for help, you better make sure you steer that player in the right direction and are always prepared to help them out. You are not "off the clock" just because you are done for the evening and a player reaches out to you for serious help. There should be no time clock on you helping that player. Always keep in mind what is important in life and be sure your baseball lessons are being conducted with that idea in mind. Make sure you link up with a coach or instructor who is willing to go the extra mile for you and can teach on that three-dimensional level. Be sure the coach gives you advice to not only help you in baseball, but to help you in life so you know he cares about you and your future.

E. Grand Slam—*Mike Just's Story*

> *It's kind of fun to do the impossible.*
> —Walt Disney

Personal Baseball Memoirs

Here are some short vignettes from my baseball life that I hope will encourage and inspire you.

Overcoming Adversity

From my journal:

....

Today is Sunday, May 15, 2005, and it may be my greatest lesson I learned to this point in my life. To overcome pain, to overcome negativity and prove to myself I can do whatever I set my mind to is nothing more than the truth and I believe Einstein has a theory that proves this as well. How many times has it been said that you can do whatever you set your mind to. It is also written in Scripture that, "I can do all things through Christ who gives me strength" (Phil. 4:13).

But does one truly believe it?

Right, right . . . if I want to become a baseball player I just have to put my mind to it, and wham! I can do it. It seems simple enough, but how many people can wholeheartedly believe it. This simple real life situation proves that if you believe you can accomplish something, you will accomplish it.

0-for-8 . . . that's how I started my three-game conference series, but I wasn't in the basic slump. I was struggling badly with my mental approach, and there were a lot of factors that had to do with it. One of the many was a misunderstanding with one of my teammates, which began the mental anguish and it snowballed from there. To add to it, the last couple of games my knee was bothering me a lot. I did not want to go to our trainer, mostly because I wasn't in the mood to wake up early for treatment, and then stay after games for more treatment. I played the first couple of games with the knee constantly nagging. On top of the knee, I had a situation going on with my cousin at the field that my coach called me to ask if I would intervene. Worried about the outcome of that situation, I played my second game just as poorly as the first game. So poorly, in fact, that the umpire honestly said he had never seen me swing that bad in my three years here.

After that second game, my body was drained, but most of all, I had lost it mentally.

Too much stuff was building up, and during all of this, my knee was pissing me off. I went to the trainer after the second game and told her that my knee hurt and that I probably couldn't play tomorrow. This was the first time I said something like that my entire college career. She took me seriously and ran some tests and concluded that my knee either had tendinitis, or there was a slight fracture in my upper shin causing the pain. The only way to find out the cause would be to take some time off or run some tests at the hospital and she said preferably both. She said if it is a slight fracture, I would be done for the season, and if it is tendinitis, I would have to rest it, or play if I am capable. She went into the Coach's Room (as it's called) and told Coach my situation that I could not play tomorrow. He was caught off guard, and told her that he would speak to me in the morning.

As I came out of the clubhouse, now I had a truthful reasoning as to why I went 0-for-8. I had a bum knee, which was all true, but it fit the circumstance. My family was concerned, and I told them that I would not play tomorrow even though it was an important game that was for placing in the conference. They said they understood, and decided that they would leave early in the morning then. I was upset, but I told myself, "Hey, I'm injured, so it's okay to take some time off to rest."

I went home that night, and Phil Laurent, my fellow teammate/ friend, who I lived in an apartment with, asked me how my knee was doing. I told him my situation and the possible outcomes and he kind of just stood there smirking. Phil and I have lived in the same apartment for three years. He reads me like a book. He continued to ask me, "How much does it really hurt?"

I told him that it was painful and that it was hindering my swing, which was the truth. I just told him, "Look at the results of the past two games. I can't swing right because of my knee, so this is the best situation right now."

Phil continued to say, "Well you know what Mike, I have dealt with injuries all year, yet I have played through them."

I replied, "Well that's good for you man, but this one is hindering my swing."

He surprisingly struck back hard, "No it's not. You're letting it and you're softer than I thought."

I leaned against the wall and thought about it for a moment.

He continued, "You hit excellent in batting practice, and you're telling me it is hindering your swing! Just because you made out eight times doesn't mean that your knee is the cause."

I replied, "Well, I'm telling you that it bothers me and it is the cause. (Deep down I wondered and thought that maybe I could stick it out tomorrow and play. It probably was just tendinitis and yes it would bother me, but not much more than it has been the past couple of weeks. I knew that I was drained mentally, and this was an easy solution to run from reality.)

Phil replied calmly, "Mike, look . . . we need you tomorrow. If it is so bad that you cannot swing with it, then don't play. But if you think you can gut it out, then do it. Because personally, I want you out there and our team as a whole would be better if you were, so just think about it." He continued, "You know what Mike, this is perfect and I'll tell you why. You are in a situation where you can run and hide, or you can face your adversity. I know what you have been going through the past few days and there is a lot on your mind. But, I would like to see you prove to yourself that when the going gets tough, you won't think of an easy way out, but rather face the problems and accomplish what you set your mind to. Mentally, you checked out after your first at-bat on Friday. I saw it in your eyes. Prove to yourself that you can face this challenge, and that the pain in your knee is mostly in your mind."

I responded with something that backed up Phil's point. I said, "You know what Phil, I don't know a lot of things anymore. I am questioning a lot and going through a lot. In fact, I can't even tell if my knee hurts more mentally, or physically."

He said, "Then there you go. You know what to do Mike and look at it this way, if you call Coach or the trainer tomorrow morning and they say that they definitely want you to sit even though you tell them that you think you can play, then there is nothing more you can do, but be content that you attempted to face your problems rather than run from them. But, if you do play tomorrow and you go 0-for again, no need to worry, because then you have accomplished something on a much larger scale that you have struggled with all of your life. So whether you get a hit or not, you will be content with your effort."

I went over to Phil, with tears in my eyes and gave him a big hug. That's a friend, and I am lucky to have one like that who cares to that extent and put me in my place when I need it.

Many people never have that fortunate experience and they deal with issues that they are never made aware of the rest of their life.

I called the trainer the next morning and told her that I could play. I briefly told her that it was just as much mental as it was physical, and I could overcome it. She said that it would ultimately be my decision since she doesn't know what it is at this point, nor does she know my pain tolerance. She informed me to call Coach and talk to him. I called him, but got his machine. I left him a lengthy message that I could play. I headed over to the field early to get treatment on the knee. There I was greeted by our coach and he asked how I was doing which he's never done before. I told him that the knee bothered me, but I could stick it out. He assured me that we actually already clinched a spot in the tournament, so it wasn't necessary for me to play, even though he would like to pick up a win today for ranking purposes in the tournament. I said, "Okay Coach, I can play today."

Coach said, "Well I don't want you to be a tough guy on me and hurt yourself for the tournament. I understand you're hurt because you rarely complain about injuries. I made two lineups, one with you in it, and one with you out of it. Take batting practice and let me know how you feel, and we'll go from there."

I felt good about that plan and also that Coach and I were on the same page. He left the room with the trainer to discuss the situation. It was definitely one of the closest moments I felt with my college head coach in all four years.

During batting practice I focused on driving the ball. I didn't pay any attention to my knee, and sure enough I had some good rounds of batting practice. Our assistant coach, who was throwing, gave me a positive, "That a boy Mike! Keep swinging it like that." That fueled me more. I loved it. For the first time I felt as if the whole coaching staff was on my side and they were all being positive. Like Phil said, no matter the outcome it would be honorable and worth it.

I told one of my assistant coaches, who proceeded to tell me he had a rod put in his knee in the past, so he more than understood knee pain on a greater scale, "I guess I'll just have to hit home runs today so I can jog around the bases!" He laughed and didn't say anything in return. I got up off the bench and gave a last stretch before the start of the game. In the huddle, one of the seniors said that the scouting report on the kid is that he likes his fastball, and he will throw it consistently for the second pitch of the at-bat. I kept a mental note of that as we started the game.

I took groundballs from the first baseman and a nagging pain shot through my knee with each flex. "Who cares! Deal with it!" I told myself. Pat Gaillard, our shortstop, approached me and said,

"Hey man, thanks for playing today. Our team needs you, and your presence for leadership is needed out here in the field." I said, "Sure thing man, just help me out through the game." He replied, "Of course." We got out of the inning, and I approached the plate. I stayed positive and repeated, "No matter the outcome . . . already won." I took the first pitch, and it was a ball anyway, but the second pitch I wasted no time jumping at. I turned on a ball that was thrown on the inner half of the plate. I got jammed slightly, but I still hit it pretty well. Off the bat, it looked like it was headed right over the third base line in the air. I figured for sure it would hook foul eventually. As I slowly rounded first, I watched the ball ricochet off the foul pole and back onto the field. The umpire waved his hands in the motion of a home run. I couldn't believe it.

I jogged around the bases like I set out to do. When I crossed home, who was the first to greet me, but my roommate Phil. He looked at me and whispered as I crossed the plate, "You were full of it all along." I just laughed and said, "Thanks Phil" as I slapped his helmet. After I crossed home I was bombarded by my teammates who were extremely happy for me. Most of my family hadn't actually left yet as they had planned to, so they were cheering away in the stands. Pat Gaillard looked at me, laughed, and said, "I love you man!"

As I entered the dugout, our assistant coach said, "Hey Mike, I didn't know you were serious!" I chuckled and replied, "Oh yeah, there's no way I'm running today!" He laughed.

My next at-bat didn't last long. I took the first pitch, once again a ball. As soon as I swung at the next pitch I flipped the bat and started my jog. The ball was crushed about 10 feet higher than the scoreboard in left center. The ball was hit approximately 440 feet, where one of our pitchers, Michael Schaeffer, said, "Here! Here's the ball! You hit it on the railroad tracks. Next time check for trains first before you launch one." That was the longest home

Mike pumping his Liberty team up after sliding into home safely against Coastal Carolina in the Big South Tournament. *Photo courtesy of Les Schofer and Liberty University.*

run I ever hit at Liberty. I did my jog, and when I rounded third, I murmured to our head coach, "Not running today." He shook his head with awe and actually smiled. That was hard to get him to do. When I went into the dugout our assistant coach just looked and said, "That a boy Mike," just like he said in my rounds of BP.

The trainer came over to me and said, "See, and you weren't going to play!"

Phil just walked by and smiled. I gave him another hug, and jogged out to play the field.

When I went out to the field, the umpire told me about how far the ball went on the tracks, and he took some credit for giving me some pointers in the previous game. I thanked him for that, and told him I would fly him out to the conference games myself if necessary. He laughed proudly. My next at-bat ended abruptly when I chased a low pitch and popped out to the first baseman. In my fourth at-bat, they brought in a lefty and I crushed a double down the left field line. When I reached second, Coach gave me the "take it easy sign" with his hands since we were up 9–4 at this point. I didn't have to stay on second long because Phil hit me in with a double. That was the bottom of the seventh inning.

I looked up in the stands and my mom, uncle, and cousin were clapping. I was happy, yet hurting more as the game went on. As I went to head back out to the field, my coach stopped me and asked how I was doing. I answered honestly by saying it still bothers me, but I can stick it out. At this point we had an 11–4 lead, so he said, "Good job today Mike. I'll put another player in now."

I turned toward the dugout and the team came over to pat me on the back. I was emotional, but I fought back tears. Not because of the pain, but because I had accomplished something that I never had done to this extreme before. I had faced my adversity and negativity and played one of the best games of my life. I thanked my teammates for their support, and cheered them on the rest of the game while I iced my knee.

As the game ended, I went into the locker room and over the radio they talked about the exceptional game I played. They said I was player of the game, and that I was a catalyst to the team. I looked around at my teammates and smiled.

Phil taught me a valuable lesson, yet I had to make that decision to experience it for myself. I have done what I deemed to be inevitable and I was rewarded for it no less.

It was once said that it is better to be a friend than a buddy. A buddy would agree with you because he knows it's what you want to hear. A friend is one who doesn't always tell you what you want to hear, but rather tells you what's in your best interest, and Phil is a true friend. Oh, and by the way, Phil ended up being Player of the Week that week in the conference, which was well deserved. Below is the article they released that day.

Michael Just went 3-for-4 with two home runs and a double in the 11-4 victory on Sunday. *Photo courtesy of Les Schofer and Liberty University.*

May 15, 2005·

Michael Just went 3-for-4 with two solo home runs and a double and Aaron Grijalva went 3-for-5 with a home run and a double as six players had two or more hits in the 11–4 victory.

They grabbed an early advantage in the first inning as Just (Jr., 2B, Woodcliff Lake, N.J.) would lead off the home half of the inning with his third home run of the season, off the left field foul pole, for a 1–0 lead.

The opponent would then score two in the top of the second inning to take a 2–1 advantage.

They then broke the game open in the third inning with five runs. Just again led off an inning with his second home run of the day over the left field wall. It was the second baseman's fourth of the season.

They closed out the scoring with two runs in the sixth inning. Just doubled down the left field line and Aaron would beat out an infield hit to open the inning. Phil Laurent, who went 7-for-11 in the series, then doubled to left center to score both runners. The left fielder drove in seven RBIs in the three games on the weekend.

The starter Todd Mittauer allowed four runs, three earned in six innings. The right-hander struck out four and walked three to run his record to 3–1 on the year and followed with 1 ⅔ innings of work, allowing a hit, while striking out one and walking one.

I was fortunate to have Phil Laurent to help me through that mental hurdle. Some ballplayers never get to that point or even realize they can be pushed to that level. I drew on this experience in my professional career on many occasions when I needed mental toughness the most. During a 140-game pro season, there were many nagging injuries that came along the way. I had to pick and choose my battles of what I should play with and what I shouldn't, but I found myself playing through injury more often than not without it negatively affecting my performance on the field. The incident above was the stepping stone in determining my future pain tolerance based on my mental toughness not only in baseball but also in life.

However, if a healthcare professional shuts you down from playing because your injury is serious, then there's nothing you can do and you need to accept that advice. You're entitled to a second or third opinion, but regardless, you should take the advice of the professional. If the injury is something minor and healthcare professionals have advised that you can play through if you so choose to, then I always encourage you to do so. On a lesser scale, if you have a blister and can make your own decision, keep yourself in the game and suck it up. The trainers have ice and band aids. Hopefully, this story encouraged you to press on in your adversity, no matter what it may be!

Phil Laurent and Mike Just before the start of the 2006 season. *Photo courtesy of Les Schofer and Liberty University.*

My First Opportunity . . . Sign or Don't Sign?

My college summer of 2005 I played in the NECBL for the Torrington Twisters. I hit exactly .300 and played with many exceptional players. Most were drafted, including my buddy Gordie Gronkowski . . . yes, you may know his brother "Gronk" from the NFL's New England Patriots.

After the season, I received a phone call from the Twisters GM who asked me, "Mike, do you want to play for the Mets?"

I was at the Jersey Shore crabbing, and I was in my Jeep coming back from the bait shop. I almost swerved off the side of the road when I was told this information. Not only was it the team that my family and I loved growing up as a kid, but it was incredible news . . . or was it?

There were three weeks left in the A-ball or Rookie-ball season where "The Kid" (Gary Carter) was the head coach. They needed another player for that team. Was this a good move for me or not? Here are the main circumstances I had to consider: I was coming off a great summer season and the tendinitis in my knee from that spring was all healed up. I had one year left of eligibility (my senior year), and I had to believe other pro teams would be following me because of the summer season I just had. Keep in mind, I'm also at the Jersey Shore crabbing and haven't seen live pitching in over three weeks since my season ended. So, if I got released after the three or so weeks with the Mets, then I would potentially be out of a pro future. I would have also lost my college senior year eligibility and these three weeks in pro ball would have delayed my fall semester senior year of college. The big question is, why now? Why would they want me for three weeks and now? The scout with the Mets was vague. He kept saying, they want you Mike and I need an answer by tomorrow. It sounded super sketchy.

I called my college coach and told him the details, asking for advice. His response was, "We'll win with ya or we'll win without ya." Nice . . . not the response I needed or was looking for. I called other players from Liberty who had been in similar situations before to get their feedback. Most of them said it doesn't sound like a real opportunity for you, Mike. It sounds like something's up and I would try to find out more information before making that commitment. I went with the majority and, as hard as it was, I turned down the opportunity. I said to the scout, "Thank you very much for the opportunity. I have to believe there will be more after this senior season is finished where I can have a chance to perform over the course of a whole season and not for three weeks. Thank you anyway and I will stay in touch."

My dad asked (now current Mets third base coach) Tim Teufel that following year if he felt I made the right decision concerning the Mets and he was almost positive that I made the right move. (Tim's son Shawn played at Liberty with me.) However, we still never had a definite confirmation of whether I, without a shadow of a doubt, made the right call.

Four years later, in 2009, I would find out for sure.

I was in spring training with the Atlantic League for the Blue Crabs, and I happened to be sitting next to Gary Carter eating lunch.

He was a coach of another team in the league called the Long Island Ducks. I introduced myself and he said, "I know who you are Mike. Great job last year for the Bears."

I was pumped that he knew me, but I played it sort of cool until I replied, "My dad, as a diehard Mets fan, would be going nuts right now if he knew I was sitting next to you having lunch."

Then someone walked up behind me with a plate of food and said, "Then tell your dad we both say hi."

Picture taken during 2009 Blue Crabs preseason. *Photo courtesy of Joseph Novak/JCN Digital Photography.*

It was Bud Harrelson. I chuckled and said, "Hey Buddy! You were one heck of a shortstop!" He said sarcastically, "Mike please don't flatter me. If you total my numbers lefty and righty at the plate I'm still pretty sure I don't reach your numbers."

I laughed and replied, "Bud stop! Wow I'm speechless and very much appreciate that. Thank you both for all that you have done for baseball."

They shrugged it off in a cool way as if they've been told that line a thousand times and proceeded to eat. I then brought up to "The Kid" the predicament I was in back in 2005. I asked him, "Do you remember when you were coaching that A-ball or Rookie-ball team for the Mets back in 2005? You had a need for a second baseman for three weeks. Do you remember why you needed him?

He laughed and said, "Tell me that guy was you."

I laughed and said, "Yes it was and I'm trying to still figure out if I made the right call or not by not signing."

He put his fork down with food still on it, leaned in to me staring intensely, and said, "You absolutely made the right decision. Our infielder broke his leg on a double play turn and he was rehabbing to come back. We needed a roster spot fill-in and then odds are that you were going to be released after that season since the other player would have had the offseason to heal. Therefore, you made the right decision."

Ahhh . . . closure and it turns out it was the right call after all!

Most people would never have the opportunity to receive that information and would always be wondering, "If only." I felt blessed and encouraged in that moment.

My "Cup of Coffee" with the Houston Astros

I did all the little things right. Showed up early, left late. I wasn't going to do anything stupid that would mess this opportunity up. I knew I had to produce. The time is now and there's no room for error. I had just finished the best season of my pro career, Rookie of the Year in the Northern League, and I was the only guy in that lineup who hadn't played affiliated baseball yet. In fact, the whole lineup except me was stacked with former triple-A guys. So, when Houston put me with the intended High-A players in spring training, I thought I was more than prepared.

The month of March came and went, and sure enough I was hitting .350, had just stolen my 10th base without being caught once, and hadn't committed a single error at third base the entire month. They pulled me up to run with the big leaguers twice. The coaches nicknamed me "Anama Secreto" (Secret Weapon in

PHOTO COURTESY OF MIKE JUST

Woodcliff Lake resident Mike Just is preparing to join the Houston Astros in Kissimmee, Fla., for spring training.

The Bergen Record featured Mike when he signed his professional contract. *Photo courtesy of Anthony and JoAnn Just.*

Spanish). Keith Bodie, our hitting coach, kept telling me, "You're doing great and you remind me so much of myself." I was super confident and felt like I could do no wrong.

When we played against the Nationals in spring training, I got a hit off of major-league pitcher Ray King, and guess who happened to be the coach of that team: former major leaguer Randy Tomlin, who was the most loved and respected coach from Liberty

Mike (#68) with his Astros teammates in spring training, 2008. *Photos courtesy of Anthony Just.*

when I was there. It was great to see him again, and this time we were in different dugouts. He hugged me and said, "I'm glad you've made it here and you're looking really good. I wish you all the best."

The last day of cuts the "clubby" (clubhouse manager) walks around with the black card. When he puts it in your locker that means you have a meeting and then you're released. He stopped at my locker and put a black card in it. A bunch of my teammates stared at me. I could tell they were shocked because I made a solid impression in the short amount of time there and I was starting to become more of a leader in the locker room. I thought maybe they just wanted to talk about a few things.

I went down to the meeting and there sat a few people who weren't the managers that had been encouraging me on the field. These two sat me down and said, "Mike, you did great! You proved to be one of our best hitters and infielders we have from top to bottom. The problem is that we have set guys in certain spots and certain money invested in certain areas and there's nothing we can do. It just comes down to numbers and none of those guys are hurt, so . . . we have to release you. You did everything you could."

In that moment I felt a variety of emotions and none were good.

This was the biggest moment of my life coming to a close and, up until that point in my career, I had never been cut from a baseball team. Anger, tears, helplessness, bitterness, disbelief . . . you name it and I felt it in that moment.

I couldn't say anything at all. What does one say that can be of any good? I shook their hands and softly muttered, "Thank you," and headed right into the bathroom and broke down. I must have cried in that stall for at least five minutes before I got my bearings together to head to the clubhouse to get my stuff.

I went into the locker room and I was greeted by a few guys whom I stay in touch with today. Matt Cusick was a second baseman in their organization that should have made it to the major leagues. He was traded when his scout was fired by Houston, and then Matt was released from that other organization after getting hit in the helmet and suffering a minor concussion. Instead of giving him some time, they wasted no time releasing him. He ended up calling me two years later for help and I helped him get a contract with the Blue Crabs in the Atlantic League.

Chris Frey, who hit .299 his first year in pro ball, was released for no reason other than no one could find a roster spot for him, either. Those guys embraced me and let me cry on their shoulders for probably another five minutes. Both said the same thing: "If Houston doesn't want you, a classy player who works hard and produces, then they may as well cut us all." Sure enough not only did many players go, so did those that released us. The uppers cleaned house in the Astros administration that year.

I will never forget how those two players (Matt and Chris) embraced me in that moment and helped build me back into that team thought process, even if it was only for another few minutes. I watched them walk out to the field and I packed up my stuff (whatever was left of it because the clubby took back what the organization wanted while I was in the meeting) and I got in the car and called my parents. Then, I contemplated Disney World while I was down there, but there was no way I could remotely enjoy it. I started the long drive from Orlando, Florida (ironically the place I was when I first received the call and the place I have always associated with Disney's laughter and enjoyment), back to New Jersey.

It was a tough time for me, but I would bounce back and sign a contract in the Atlantic League, which was and still is the best Independent league in the world. All major leaguers who get released and still play on will try to play in that league. Something spectacular would happen in my last season in pro ball of 2009. A moment fit for the Hollywood screens and now that you have gone this far in my career with me (to continue the *Shawshank* reference) and shared in some of my joy, pain, and sorrow, maybe you are ready for one last story. . . .

Mike after he launches a home run to left. *Photo courtesy of Joseph Novak/JCN Digital Photography.*

The Best Day in My Pro Career

The best day of my professional career is something I'm proud of. There have been other eventful moments in my career, but none that can surpass the array of emotion I felt during the 2009 Atlantic League All-Star Game.

My career has been a movie to say the least. You see, playing in Independent ball to most players is a letdown, because they were already in the majors, or they were knocking on the door, or they received their signing bonus and expected big things, yet before they knew it they were back to square one . . . fighting once again for an opportunity.

For me, playing Indy ball was *the* opportunity. When I received a call in July 2006 to play for the River City Rascals in the Frontier League, opportunity rang.

A game shot of Mike that was made into his first pro baseball card.
Photo courtesy of Don Adams Jr.

You see, out of college I wasn't drafted, yet I had the numbers to certainly achieve that honor. I broke records offensively and defensively of many who were drafted and some who even played in the major leagues.

A scout, later verified by another coach from the same school, told me that my college head coach didn't help my chances. Sadly, these things happen all the time for various reasons. I was devastated when I was told by that scout the day before the draft that I was not going to get drafted by any organization because of what was said about me. The scout turned out to be right. As a matter of fact, he felt so bad for my situation that he made a call for me and got me signed with the Rascals to start somewhere in pro ball.

After leading the Rascals in hitting in 2006, I was willingly traded to the Northern League in 2007 for five players. I was impressed, yet shocked, that some team in North Dakota thought I was worth half a starting lineup!

That year, I received Rookie of the Year honors and was signed by the Houston Astros. But as you already know, it didn't pan out.

Devastated from that, I called up the Newark Bears, who saw me at a tryout in Florida with the Philadelphia Phillies. At that tryout, I went 6-for-9 with two stolen bases and was told by a Phillies scout that I could not field and throw. Did he know I had the assists record at my four-year college? Did he also know that I only committed 10 errors my entire college career at second base and owned the single-season hit record? How about the fact that I only made 23 errors in over 360 games of playing second and third base in pro ball? That's about only an error every 16 games, but I can't field right?

Well, Coach "Chick" Krenchicki and the Bears thought otherwise!

Mike Just hits a home run for the Fargo-Moorhead RedHawks in the Northern League. *Photo courtesy of Mike and Linda Jones.*

Mike backhands a ball at third and throws the runner out at first. *Photo courtesy of Newark Bears Organization.*

They gave me an opportunity and started me Opening Day at third base.

I couldn't believe I was playing among the players I had pitched and hit with in video games. I was honored to be on the same field as them, but you better believe when I stepped in the box that their life was not going to be easy. I would make them work to get the "no-named" Just guy out. The season was going well and I was hitting around .295 at the All-Star break. Not long after that, a major leaguer was brought in to play third. I found myself on the bench. Chick gave me an option. He said I could stay and get in here and there, or I could get traded to a team in any Independent league of my choice and I would start every day. It seemed like a no-brainer to me. I knew I couldn't get signed if I wasn't playing, so I decided I needed to take the other opportunity and play every day.

Before I went in to talk to Chick, Benito Baez (a pitcher for the Bears and strong Christian man of faith) asked me if I prayed about the situation. I am also a Christian, but in this situation I figured what was there to pray about? It seemed pretty obvious to me. I have to take the opportunity right? Well I decided to pray and I felt a strong peace about staying on the team. We had a daily Bible study group and I was helping some guys out with their life situations. I went in and told Chick, and he said he would be honored to have me as a backup.

The rest of the 2008 season I didn't play much. As a matter of fact, my average suffered because of it. But is the most important thing in life someone's batting average, or the difference one makes in someone else's life? Not long after that Bears season ended, a player from the Bears turned his life around because of our daily talks on the team. It seemed as if God had a plan all along.

Photo courtesy of Joseph Novak/JCN Digital Photography.

During the offseason I wasn't sure if I should play the 2009 season. I called teams in the Atlantic League, but no one was interested. With one week to go before the start of spring training, Butch Hobson and the Southern Maryland Blue Crabs traded for my rights to get me aboard. I was ecstatic! Not only was that the team I wanted to play for, but also my fiancée lived 45 minutes from that field in Maryland.

My motto from the start of the season was to *"have fun and enjoy each day as it may be your last."* Over the past years that I played in pro ball, I was always trying to make it up to the next level and I was forgetting to enjoy my time at hand. My approach would now be different. The season started off well and I was

Photo courtesy of Joseph Novak/JCN Digital Photography.

confident I was going to prove everyone wrong and do something great.

Around the All-Star break I had great numbers! I thought that I had a shot at making the All-Star team. When the ballots were released and my name was left off, I was disappointed. I discussed the matter with our announcer Paul Braverman, and he said that it was completely ridiculous! He gave me hope because he told me I could get enough write-in votes to still get in. Based on the odds, I figured my "opportunity" was dwindling. I played each game hard and hoped and prayed for votes. When Butch sat me down and told me one-on-one that I'm not going to believe this but I had enough write-in votes to make the All-Star team, I was in shock. I told him about how I always get screwed in those situations and how I was so thankful I was going! He responded with, "Not this year. I'm your manager now."

What a relief to hear that! My manager was pulling for me! The All-Star Game took place in Newark, New Jersey. I live 25 minutes north of there. I had a block of 50 tickets set aside for my friends and family to attend and every ticket was accounted for. I knew that this could be something great. My whole career had been some version of a letdown up until this point.

Carpe Diem came to mind when I was warming up in left field. Could I seize the day?

I figured players and scouts might think, "The little Just kid who never had an affiliated at-bat should just be thankful he's even here."

Perhaps that crossed my mind, too, but also what if? What if I take full advantage of this day and do everything right? Would I get signed? Is it even about that anymore? It's about much more than a little political contract that my career turned into. It's about proving my right to play against major-league players and making them remember the little Just kid . . . respect.

Upon my arrival, celebrities by the dozens poured into the stadium for a celebrity softball game before the All-Star Game main event. I got to meet and talk with most of them:

Frank Vincent—actor. *Photo courtesy of Mike Just.*

D'Brickashaw Ferguson—New York Jets offensive tackle. *Photo courtesy of Mike Just.*

Ozzie Smith—aka "The Wizard" . . . enough said. *Photo courtesy of Mike Just.*

Justin Tuck—New York Giants defensive end. *Photo courtesy of Mike Just.*

Queen Latifah—rapper/actress/comedian. *Photo courtesy of Mike Just.*

Angie Martinez—rapper/actress. *Photo courtesy of Mike Just.*

Mayor (and future senator) Corey Booker and dozens more celebrities were present too.

When the celebrity softball game ended, our game was breezing by. It was the fifth inning and we were losing, but not by much. I remember thinking that I have at least two more at-bats in the game. What if? What if the game is on the line and I get up? If the score remains close, they will bring in none other than Armando Benitez . . . the pitcher I rooted for as a kid. Growing up I remember thinking, it's a good thing I don't have to face that guy. Now I was thinking, that could be my moment to get MVP of this All-Star Game and shock my detractors. But what are the odds everything would fall into place for that to happen?

Before I knew it I was on deck in the top of the ninth.

We were down two runs with runners on second and third with Benitez on the mound. I knew my friends and family were rooting for the same moment. They knew my career, they knew the letdowns, they wanted me to succeed.

A friend of mine recommended I read *The Art of War* by Sun Tzu. It discusses how to outsmart your opponent via strategic maneuvers in war. It also tells you to be more prepared than your competition. In the battle of "David vs. Goliath," as one article put my encounter with Benitez, I was ready. Watching him throw as a child, knowing his aggression is a sign of weakness when he gets rattled, even throwing with him in video games . . . I was prepared. Knowing how all 5'10" of me (with cleats on) looks walking into the box, even with a base open, he was going to come after me. Sometimes size can be an advantage if you can plan accordingly.

I was up with two outs. I had visualized this moment an hour ago in the field. I had known I was more prepared than he was as I stepped into that box. I knew this moment for me was a hundred times more than the moment for him (given where he had been and what he had accomplished).

I was ready.

First pitch . . . fastball, ball one.

He snapped at the ball with his glove when the catcher returned the ball back to him. Based on his frustration after that pitch, I figured that he wasn't trying to throw a ball. Therefore, I stuck with what I had originally thought; he was trying to go after me, regardless of the open base.

Next pitch . . . fastball, ball two.

Men are on base and the tying run is at second.

He knows this, and wants to go after me.

Next pitch . . . fastball, ball three!

Could I have over-analyzed the situation?

Was he pitching around me?

Now I stepped out of the box to take a breather and re-gather my thoughts. I'm not going to second-guess myself. The moment is here. I'm sticking with the original plan. He's going after me and I'm not walking. I step in and wait for the 3–0 delivery.

Strike! It was about two inches off the outside corner. Had I made any gestures to go to first, the ump might have granted me the walk because good umpires can read the hitter's body language on close pitches. Instead, I stayed in the box as if I knew it was a strike all along because I wanted to hit. I was destined for this moment. I re-gathered myself under control and waited for the 3–1 fastball.

The pitch was on its way and it was hittable.

I took a swing and swung right through it. At least I thought it was hittable because I was sitting dead red fastball. It was a 3–1 slider. As a hitter, if you convince yourself that a certain pitch is coming, you can almost change the look of the pitch halfway to the plate believing that you are right . . . that is until reality sets in and it moves in a different direction.

Now it was a 3–2 count.

Runners were still on second and third with two outs in the top of the ninth.

He had thrown a slider on 3–1? The slider wasn't even his best pitch. His diving split complements his 94-mph sinking fastball exceptionally well.

I stepped back into the box with the 3–2 count. I was now thinking slider, but was ready to foul off the fastball if he went with it. It was a good plan because of Benitez's experience. He just saw me look foolish on the 3–1 slider and would most likely throw something off-speed again.

The pitch was on its way. I recognized it and instantly thought, not a fastball . . . wait . . . wait . . . swing! Foul ball! He threw me a 3–2 splitter.

Now I had him right where I wanted him and here's why. I showed him I'm waiting on his off-speed pitch when I fouled off that splitter. Meanwhile, I have yet to swing at one of his fastballs. He knows I'm not a power guy and has no reason to throw three off-speed pitches to me in a row when he throws a sinking fastball at 94 mph and there are dozens of scouts in the stands with radar guns observing the moment.

I stepped out and when I stepped back in the box, I stepped a half inch farther out from the plate than I had previously set up. It was enough for me to notice a difference, but not enough for the catcher or Benitez to notice. I did this because, when he throws that fastball, I want to make sure I stay inside of it. If it's sinking hard in on my hands, if I try and pull the sinking fastball, I will most likely ground out. I was playing the odds and I was ready for the 3–2 pitch.

Benitez released the ball and it was a fastball that started on the inner third of the plate and was running toward the inside corner. I kept my hands inside of it and barreled a line drive single up the middle scoring both runners!

I had done it!

My friends and family were going crazy! I could hear them for the first time all game because I had zoned them out to focus. But, I quickly regained my focus because I knew my job wasn't done. The game was only tied.

Knowing Benitez and how rattled he must have been at this point, I took the liberty of stealing second on the first pitch, figuring that he was focused in on getting the hitter out. I stole it standing up.

Former major leaguer Luis Lopez was up, and on the next pitch, he ripped a liner to left and I scored the go-ahead run.

We ended up pushing across one more run that inning, and when major leaguer Bill Simas came in to close out the game, I felt I had captured the opportunity.

Could I get the MVP?

As we shook hands I heard guys saying to me, "Great job MVP!" I had a flashback.

In high school, I hit two home runs in one game in the County Tournament, which tied a county record. They walked me three times in the championship game, one time on four pitches with the bases loaded. When it came time for MVP of the tournament, all the guys were cheering my nickname (Mr. Automatic) and saying you got it for sure. Soon after, they announced a pitcher as the MVP for making a certain amount of appearances. I was dejected. Would this happen to me again?

As I got to the end of the line, Andre Rabouin (pitching coach) and Butch Hobson pulled me aside and said wait here. I knew at this point that I had done it. Soon after, league commissioner Joe Klein said congratulations to me as they were presenting the award. I remember the look on my parents' faces. My fiancée Brittany was shaking, and when we look at them today we notice all the pictures she took are blurry. My friends and the rest of my family were standing on the seats screaming. Spencer Ross, the Bears announcer, came out and presented me with the award.

They put a microphone in front of me, but I couldn't say much. I was choked up. It was a big moment for me, the biggest of my career, and I knew it right then and there.

The guys all came to hug and congratulate me. Even guys from the opposing team did the same. I overheard a pro from the other team, Vito Chiaravalloti, say to Matt Hagen (a player who previously played at Liberty), "He deserves it after what he must have been through because of his size."

If everyone only knew . . .

As the guys walked toward the clubhouse, my family and friends were still there roaring! I held the crystal cup up and yelled to them, "I did it!"

As I walked toward my family, the Bears general manager, Mark Skeels, stopped me to say, "Walt Disney could not have written this story better. Congratulations Mike!"

*None of the pictures below were taken by my family or friends. They were too busy celebrating.

Andre Rabouin (#12) and Butch Hobson (#17) pull me aside. *Photo courtesy of Joseph Novak/JCN Digital Photography.*

At a loss for words with Spencer Ross. *Photo courtesy of Joseph Novak/ JCN Digital Photography.*

Former Yankees and pro sports team announcer Stan Ross with MVP Mike Just. *Photo courtesy of Joseph Novak/JCN Digital Photography.*

Holding up the crystal cup to my friends and family. *Photo courtesy of Joseph Novak/JCN Digital Photography.*

Mike gets acquainted with Armando Benitez for the first time before the game starts!

Now that you have heard my story, I shall add that, to my knowledge, I was the only player in the history of the Atlantic League to technically never have an official affiliated at-bat, yet gain the MVP of the All-Star Game . . . and guess what . . . I'm damn proud of it.

So, what happened next you might ask?

Why didn't more teams call or more opportunities come up?

Well, one did for Armando Benitez . . . he was signed and put back in Triple A with none other than the Houston Astros a few weeks after that game.

What can you do but laugh sometimes, but I was still happy for him regardless. Good for him!

I was fortunate to have been blessed with the opportunity, and I'm thankful to all of my friends and family who supported me along the way for all of those years. My baseball experiences gave me the confidence to propel Just Hits, my baseball academy, into what it is today and influence players' lives for the better, and you can't beat that.

For most of us, life is never meant to be easy. It's a grind and takes hard work. In the grand scheme of things, as hard as the path was and as hard as life is, I've been blessed with many baseball memories that I will hold on to always. Regardless if they were "just" memories or not, I hope you build your own lifelong memories, and achieve opportunities for success in this great game we call baseball.

The framed picture below still hangs at Regency Furniture Stadium in the main office of the Southern Maryland Blue Crabs. They made two and gave me one as a gift for the accomplishment.

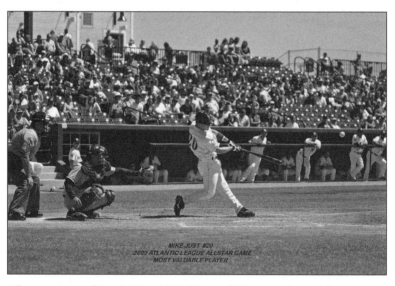

Photo courtesy of Joseph Novak/JCN Digital Photography and the Southern Maryland Blue Crabs Professional Baseball Team.

SOURCES

Newspapers and Magazines

The Bergen Record
201 Magazine

Websites

www.drugabuse.gov
www.mlb.com
www.livestrong.com
www.valleyleaguebaseball.com
http://www.liberty.edu/flames
www.functionalmovement.com
www.ncaa.com
www.statsstylescore.com

ACKNOWLEDGMENTS

A very special thanks goes out to each one of you for somehow playing a role in making this book dream a reality. Much love to you all! Scott Brosius, Rob Skead, George McGovern, Rich Guenther, Debbie Soriero, David Lamanna, Aaron Sabato, James Airo, Kathy Perry, JoAnn Just, Dr. Anthony Just, Dr. Robert Just, Ryan Page, Danielle Carr, Austin Schimmel, Lara DiNatale, Jared Strasser, Nick Levy, Brian Leonard, and Crosland Stuart.